MW01612157

Decisions
Decisions
Decisions

Phillip Adams, O.D.

Stephenville, Texas

DECISIONS, DECISIONS, DECISIONS
© 2004 By Phillip Adams

Published by Rhizoo Publishing.
P.O. Box 1249
Stephenville, Texas 76401

Unless otherwise indicated, Scripture quotations used in this book are from the New International Version. 1996, ©1984 Grand Rapids: Zondervan.

Scripture quotations indicated as NKJV are from the New King James Version. 1996, ©1982. Nashville: Thomas Nelson.

Scripture quotations indicated as KJV are from the King James Version. 1995. Oak Harbour, WA: Logos Research Systems. Inc.

Quotation of Mike Hayes, *When God is First,* reprinted by permission.

Emphasis in all quotations are the author's.

Throughout this book, the plural of the word *kairos* will be designated by the word *kairos'*.

ISBN 0-9762723-0-X

Printed in the United States of America

Dedication

I did not realize at the onset of this project that the most difficult part would be the dedication page. Oh, it is not difficult in the sense of having difficulty making a choice. It is difficult only in this. My life ... where I am in this world ... and where I am with God can not be attributed to any one person. My life has been bettered and enriched by so many people. And when I make this dedication, those people ... my wife ... family ... friends and ministers, must all be left out. They fail to be recognized for who they are to me. I hope I have been faithful to let each of you know how important you are in my life.

I dedicate this work to the two
loveliest Servants of God that I
know. I dedicate it to the couple
into whose lives and home I was
birthed and nurtured and cared for —
spirit, soul, and body.
I dedicate it to my parents,
James and Millie Adams.

You are Two Oak Trees ...
for the Kingdom of God ...
and for me.

I thank God for giving me the honor of calling you
Mom and Dad.

Table of Contents

CHAPTER 1

The Concept

I wish I could say this was a novel. I wish I had that almost mystical ability to draw imaginary events gently out of their shadowy world of possibility and make them live. I wish my mind was plagued with characters having rich lives, some obscure but others prominent, waiting to join one another on pages that marched toward the climax of a crisis, real or imagined. But if I have that ability, I have not yet learned how to harness it—at least not in the style of someone like, say, Frank E. Peretti.

It has been more than a dozen years since I first read a Peretti novel. And I suspect that he wouldn't mind me saying that if you have never read one, you should. I would suggest one of his "Darkness" novels. In his works, Mr. Peretti masterfully ties events past to events present ... and future. He creates realistic ties between subtle events in unheard of lives and monumental events in the lives of people he causes us to know well. He illuminates the spirit world as brightly as though it were the natural. And he takes all these elements and weaves them into a tale—a tale that accelerates its way toward a pinpoint of time. A point of time where we can only guess what *will* happen, or what *might possibly* happen, or what *we want* to happen. We are tempted to jump ahead, but dare not for fear of missing out on a detail that is key to the final outcome of the book.

If what I have written here causes you to put this book down and to take up one of his, I hope that when you have finished it you will return to this one, because there is a tie between the two. This book deals with those climactic points of life where things happen. Battles take place in the spirit world and events are molded in the natural. The course of individual lives (and sometimes groups of lives) are changed, or determined, at those pinpoints of time. And while the specifics in Mr. Peretti's books are fictional, I suspect most of us will never know—at least not in this life and realm—how close to accurate those descriptions may turn out to be. But what I *do* know, and what we *can* discover from a close exploration of the Bible, is that individuals, churches, communities, nations and even the world march continually in the direction of pinpoints of time where destinies are determined. These moments fill the scriptures. They are crossroads in time and space—places where the spirit world interacts with the natural. They are the times in individual and human history where a timeless God conducts the business of carrying out His plan for a timed mankind. They are moments of decision ... moments of opportunity ... or in the Greek—*kairos* moments.

Somewhere in my past, before I even learned the word *kairos*, I began to wonder about those moments. You may have heard someone say, "She missed a golden opportunity," or "He was at the right place at the right time." Have you ever wondered about those "opportunities" or "times"? Do you ever wonder about why things turn out the way they do, or how people got to where they are, either because things seem good for them, or maybe bad? I do. I guess I'm an incurable ponderer, because I wonder about everything. And sometimes it gets in the way of accomplishing a task ... but sometimes it helps. I wonder about the "what if's" of life ... and the "why's." Do you ever stop to think about those? For instance, have you ever wondered, "How did we get here?" I don't mean how did we human beings get here. I don't mean, "What are our origins?" I mean you and I. How is it that you and I have ended up here together, sharing time and thoughts for awhile through the pages of this book? And how did we come to this place where we currently find ourselves—maybe having more than the usual hunger for the Presence and direction of God in our lives? Did that hunger come about by our own efforts? And if it did, how did we create it? And could we have created it sooner? And if we could have, why didn't we? Or, is it something that was put there by the Holy Spirit? And if it was, what prompted Him to place

3

it there at this particular time rather than at some other time? Is there something that we could have done to get Him to put it there before now, rather than now?

And, I have wondered many similar things, about people I know, and about me, and about the body of Christ in general. I first began to wonder about the timing of events because of a couple of verses of scripture. Do you remember in the 8th chapter of Matthew when Jesus was visiting the land of the Gergesenes or Gadarenes and He met those two demon possessed men coming out from the tombs? What they said to Him stayed with me even after I had gone on to read other things. They asked Him, " ... Have you come here to torture us before the *appointed time*?" And then in chapter 26 of that same book Jesus said something very similar to what the demons had said. He was sending some of His disciples ahead to make preparations for all of them to spend the Passover together and He told them, " ... Go into the city to a certain man and tell him, 'The Teacher says: My *appointed time* is near....'" And it was those two verses that started me wondering about the word "time." It seemed to me as if it was saying that there is such a thing as an *appointed time* for certain things to happen. The demons knew that they had an appointed time to be tormented, and just like them, Jesus seemed to know that He had an appointed time for something in His life. Well, I say for *something*, but we know that it was for His death to occur. But the important part, as far as I was concerned that day, wasn't *what* was supposed to happen, but rather that there was such a thing as an *appointed time* for some things to happen. Those verses brought a reality into my spirit. I began to realize that *some things can only happen at certain times in our lives*, as opposed to just happening at any random time.

As this realization was birthed, I fed it. I went to a concordance and a variety of other resources where I found the Greek roots for the word "time." I discovered other words that were similar, but not the same. I learned that there are actually at least three words in the New Testament that are sometimes translated into the word "time." I read about all three of them, but I soon realized that I would not need to spend too much *time* (figure it out for yourself which of the three I mean here) on two of the words. Nor will I as I describe what I discovered. The first, and most easily grasped of the Greek words was *aion,* which is pretty easy for us English speakers, because it still sounds the same today. It is our word *eon*, which, of course, just means ages or very lengthy periods of time. The next was *chronos* which is also a word to describe an indefinite (but usually shorter than an eon) period of time. But the one that intrigued me, the one that caused me to write this book, was very different from the first two. It was the word *kairos*, which I mentioned earlier, and it is a much more complex word than the others. Although it can be translated to just mean *time* in the chronos sense of the word, more often than not, translating it simply as *time* does not do it justice. Unlike the other two, which deal with unspecified times, kairos more normally deals with specific *pinpoints* of time. And not only that, but the word has a quality associated with it totally apart from just a point in time. That quality makes the word more complex, so rather than just trying to define it, let me describe it for you.

A kairos time is the coming together of a necessary set of circumstances at a particular location as well as at a particular time. In fact, it is that coming together of those circumstances in a particular location that actually defines the time ... or makes it a particular or significant time. For instance, all of us have been in gatherings, reminiscing, when suddenly someone will say, "Do you remember that time when we ... ?" (Of course, we all have to fill in our own events here.) Well, it wasn't the clock or calendar that defined the time—it was the event. And we all have countless memories of that sort. For most of them, we don't remember the *actual* time ... we remember the event time, and refer to it as "that time when we...." A kairos can be *any* time where the proper circumstances come together at the right place. I think that is the reason God used it so much in the scripture. He is a timeless God and although He has a timeline with some set points on it, He largely deals with individuals by means of event timing, or kairos timing, rather than calendar timing. He provides us with kairos moments, or *moments of opportunity*, and our lives are defined by what we did ... or didn't do ... at those critical moments. These moments can vary vastly in size, importance and origin. Some of them are *almost* insignificant, others—huge. Some, both large and small, are created by God, but many others are created by us or those around us. For instance, sometimes at the ballpark they will declare it to be a jersey night, where, say, the first twenty-five thousand people with a paid admission get a free team jersey. Well, a couple of things have to be in place if you want that free jersey. First, you have to be at the right place. You may have already bought and paid for a ticket, but if you don't show up at the park, you don't get your jersey. And then, of course, you have to get there at the right time—somewhere between person one and person twenty-five thousand. If you are number 25,001 all that your ticket will get you is admission to the game. You miss your jersey. But, if you buy a ticket and get there at the appropriate time, you hit the jersey kairos and get the prize.

Kairos moments can be of a longer or shorter duration than that though. For instance, a radio station can create a kairos for free tickets to a concert. They can say, "Okay, be the 11th caller after you hear today's mystery sound and you will get free tickets to see...." Well, first you have to be at the right place (on your digital tuner). Then the circumstances get tougher, because you actually have to be listening in order to hear the designated sound (and we both know that just as soon as we decide to chance it and run to the bathroom, that will be when they play the sound). But it gets worse yet, because now your telephone line has to get hooked up with their switchboard between caller number ten and number twelve—a very tiny kairos indeed. It is a tough thing to do, but you can bet that someone is going to meet the requirements of that kairos. So, while these examples are trivial, I think you see what I am getting at. Some things can only happen if all the circumstances come together at the right place and at the right time—the kairos time.

As I was studying these words, I also saw some other interesting things about kairos moments. Some of them appear to be set in stone, so to speak, and others are more pliable. What I mean is this. It appears that when God, through Jesus Christ, was establishing the world—way back when He was setting the course for mankind—when He knew that His Lamb would have to be slain, He set some kairos points in place that are immovable and unchangeable. In fact, that last sentence contains one of them. Do you remember the verse that describes Jesus as "...the Lamb that was slain from the creation of the world?" Well, that can't mean that He was actually slain as the world was being founded, but rather, God saw that there would be a need for a means of redemption for His creation, and He established the "cross kairos" as a fixed point in His plan. It could not be moved or altered. That is why Jesus was able to refer to His "appointed time." There was a distinct time set for certain events in His life, including His act of redemption, and He knew it. He understood kairos moments and used the word often.

And there were many other places in the Word where God set fixed times for certain things to happen. In fact, if you think about it, on many of the occasions that God spoke to mankind through the voice of a prophet, He was establishing a set, or fixed, kairos. If that prophecy had a certain number of years associated with it, it became an immovable kairos. Many of those have already been fulfilled—right on time. Others remain in force, waiting to be fulfilled. Those would mostly be the ones regarding the end-times and the anti-Christ.

A kairos that was prophesied and came to pass right away is told about in Genesis 40. Do you remember the story of Joseph when he was in Pharaoh's prison? It was after he had refused the sexual advances of Pharaoh's wife. Well, after awhile Pharaoh sent his baker and cupbearer to prison also. Both of them had dreams and asked Joseph to try to tell them what the dreams meant. Joseph told the cupbearer that within three days he would be restored to his former position as royal cupbearer. But he told the baker that he would be executed. Now in one sense this was a prophecy to these two men. God revealed to Joseph what was about to happen, and then Joseph revealed it to the men involved. So, while God was not declaring something against the men, He knew that within three days Pharaoh was going to decide what to do about the men. He showed it to Joseph and Joseph showed it to them. What made it a kairos was that there was going to be a set of circumstances that would come together at a particular place within a given time. And, it was a set kairos, not created by God, but known to Him and revealed by Him. So while God may not have created *this particular* kairos, He *has* created the "fixed" kairos moments that were established from the beginning of the world. And He continues to create those moments in the lives of humans today. But He is not the only one who creates them (remember the jersey night where the ballpark owners created a kairos).

If all kairos moments were of the "fixed" variety, it might make us think that they were not worth our time to study, because it looks like we can't do anything about them anyway. But there are two things about these types of moments that merit a closer look. For one, what if the baker was living in New Testament times like we are and was told what he was told? His kairos time would be set, just as it was then. But knowing it ahead of time would have given him the opportunity to make some preparations. It would allow him time to give final instructions to his family. If he were not a follower of Jesus, it might provide a small window of opportunity to set his heart right with God. While he could not have done things that would have an effect on his short-term future, he would have had the opportunity to make decisions that would have effected his eternal future. And that would make the foreknowledge of a kairos inestimable in value. We can even make his story a little more relevant to our lives today like this. What if, instead of being the king's royal baker, the man had been a baker at the local doughnut shop? Instead of the king sending him to prison with a death sentence, the doctor had sent him home with the news of advanced cancer throughout his body. He only has a few weeks to live. Does the fact that the kairos of his death has been clearly established make the knowledge of that kairos unimportant? Does the fact that, in the natural, there is nothing he can do to alter his kairos by more than a few days make the knowledge of the kairos valueless? No, of course not.

In fact that knowledge lends value, and urgency, to the situation. He is only middle aged and he has a business that will need some final attention. He and his wife will want to have some tender moments together in his remaining time, just as they did in those first magical days when they fell in love. He still has children at home—children who have started on their journey with Christ, but who are not yet as firmly established as he wishes they were. He will have final words to prepare for them, to help them get a little further along their "Way" before he goes on his. And he will almost certainly have some fine tuning to do to his own walk with Christ—because while we may mean to, and want to, which one of us actually lives as close to Christ as we would if we knew we were going to meet Him face to face any day now? And lastly, while in the natural there may be nothing he can do to change his kairos, in the spirit world there may be.

Do you remember the story of Hezekiah? I find it one of the most remarkable stories in the Old Testament. It was back when Isaiah was the prophet in Israel. The story is told both in the book of Kings and in Isaiah. Hezekiah became ill and God sent Isaiah to him with this message.

> **"...Put your house in order, because you are going to die; you will not recover." (2 Kings 20:1)**

Now this wasn't just the doctor foretelling his death. It was the God of the universe, declaring in no uncertain terms that Hezekiah *would not recover*. His death kairos was set, and in a most definite way. It appeared that he only had a very short window of opportunity to do anything before his time was up.

Look how he decided to spend that time. The story is found in Isaiah 38:2-3.

> `Hezekiah turned his face to the wall
> and prayed to the LORD, "Remember,
> O LORD, how I have walked before
> you faithfully and with wholehearted
> devotion and have done what is good
> in your eyes." And Hezekiah wept
> bitterly.

And that brings up the second point about set kairos moments that I wanted to mention. While I doubt that the kairos for the appearance of the anti-Christ, or of the rapture, or of the return of Christ and the judgment of men and angels can be altered, it looks like it is possible to change some of the *personal* kairos moments that have been placed on the calendars of our lives. The reason I say that is this. Look at what God did when Hezekiah chose to spend his remaining time by turning to God with a broken and contrite heart. Isaiah 38:4 and following says:

> Then the word of the LORD came to
> Isaiah: "Go and tell Hezekiah, 'This
> is what the LORD, the God of your
> father David, says: 'I have heard your

**prayer and seen your tears; I will add
fifteen years to your life...."'**

King Hezekiah had a death kairos delivered to
him by the Creator of Heaven and Earth. Yet by turning
to God with his whole heart, he had that kairos set back
fifteen years. And who knows but what our baker
might be able to do the same thing. Great and mighty
provisions have been made for our healing. It might be
that our baker will obtain it by getting into the
Word—the source of our faith. Or maybe he will be
like Hezekiah and touch the heart of God by the
brokenness of his own heart. But the point is that just
because we may see a hard kairos before us, one that
appears to be immovable, we should not be devastated.
At the worst, it gives us time to make some positive
changes in the lives of those we will leave behind, and
at best, it gives us an opportunity to take the Kingdom
of Heaven by force, so to speak, and possibly get a
reprieve to the kairos. But it can only come about if we
see the kairos as it approaches.

Are you beginning to have a feel for these
kairos moments? Are you beginning to see their importance? We have talked about substantial kairos times.
We have also talked about the insignificant ... the
jersey, etc. But before we go on to look at how some of
our predecessors in the faith dealt with kairos moments,
we need to make one additional distinction. That
distinction is this. Kairos events are sometimes related
only to the natural world around us; at other times they
are strictly spiritual in character; and still others are

moments where the spiritual world interacts with the natural. For instance, what type of event would it be if (without having prayed about it in particular) you took a relatively low-level job with a different company, and within just a few weeks a person in a higher-level position leaves the company? You had done well in the short time that you were in your new job and upon the departure of the other person, you were moved to the higher position. This would be a kairos moment because a set of circumstances came together to create an opportune moment. You were in the right place at the right time, and because of the quality of the work you had already done, you were advanced at a quicker than normal pace. While the consequences of what happened were certainly a blessing, there was nothing overtly spiritual about this particular kairos.

Now let's envision a situation only slightly different than this. Suppose you have been a Christian for some time and you are beginning to feel that you would like to give of yourself back into the kingdom of God. You feel that if you were asked, you would be willing to teach a Sunday school class. On the other hand, you are not sure if you are ready; plus you are new in town and have only attended your church for a short while. So you put it in God's hands by telling Him that if He will cause them to ask you, rather than you asking them, you will teach. Before you even get to bed that night, the Sunday School Superintendent calls you and tells you that one of the teachers has decided to step down after fifteen years of continuous service. Someone else in the church had mentioned to the superintendent that she appreciated the spirit you demonstrated whenever she was around you and felt God wanted to use you in some way. They offer you the teaching job. This has no connection to the natural world at all. It is God intervening to confirm that what you thought was in your spirit was in fact from Him. And it was also Him intervening in a way as to create a kairos moment for you. You will be performing a spiritual duty with spiritual rewards ... a spiritual kairos.

So, what about the spirit world interacting with the natural. There is a really interesting example in the Bible. You can read about it in Numbers 22. Let me change that—you *need* to read about it even if you are already familiar with the story. I went back to re-read it for myself, and as I did, I realized that although I recognized it as a kairos moment, I had never read it strictly from that perspective. Doing so added a whole new layer of depth to the story. Let me mention the event here, but before you go much further go read the story. It is only one chapter long. In Numbers 22 you will read about a king named Balak, a prophet named Balaam, a burro named Burrito (well maybe not) ... but a burro, and an angel of God. Balak and Balaam were essentially components of the natural world, the angel was of the spirit world and the burro became an interface between the two worlds. In this account, the invisible angel first becomes visible to the donkey and then to Balaam. It was a kairos in the history of the Jewish people, and in the life of Balaam, and now that I think about it, in the life of the donkey. But because the event involved an angel of God sent to manifest himself to the natural world, it was a kairos of both a natural and a spiritual character.

Kairos moments. Some are almost insignificant; some are monumental. Some deal with the physical world, some with the spiritual, and some with both. In our lives, both in the natural and the spiritual, these crossroads represent moments of opportunity. They can be brief, set moments—or they can be longer and more flexible (both are equally important). They can be, at the very least, prepared for—and possibly even altered. They can be created by God, by others, or even by our own actions and decisions. And what we do, or don't do, at these crucial times can effect our destiny. In fact, *they define our destiny.*

CHAPTER 2

How It Works

There is a bittersweet verse in the Bible. I am glad that God hasn't placed a limit on the number of times that any one person can use any one verse ... because I have worn this verse out. When I think about the comfort that I have taken from the verse—when I dig back through the many ruins in my past, and the rubbish piles—I find its impact everywhere. When I think of the strength that the verse carries, and how it has bolstered me when I needed it most, my eyes well up. When I find my heart to be less tender than I like, I think of how I have used the verse, and how its words have seemed to call out, "I'm here for such a time as this; let me do what you can't," and I am softened. It has shined light into deep gloom, and even despair. It has protected a wisp of irrational hope when everything about me shouted destruction. I would never say that it is my favorite verse—not my life verse ... only my most used—and I hope that I never need to use it again—or even read it, or go to sleep with it rolling through my mind and spirit.

Why would I want to be able to forget about a verse that has carried me through so many of the rough spots in my life? Well, *that is why*—I only find it in the rough spots of my life. And if I never need the verse again it will mean that I have avoided those hard times yet to come. The verse is Romans 8:28.

> **And we know that in all things God works for the good of those who love him, who have been called according to his purpose.**

And knowing that verse, and using that verse, and having great confidence in that verse has been of inestimable value to me over the years of my mistakes and trials. So while I know that trials will continue in this life, and I know that God can and will work some good out of the bad, I am in hopes that I can begin to avoid some of the mistakes.

I have discovered that just because God is able to salvage some good out of my blunders doesn't mean that those mistakes were desirable, or that they were the will of God for my life. It just means that He is gracious and powerful and loves me. He uses those attributes of His character that are able to keep the disasters of my life from being a total waste. He makes it so that the sorrow that comes my way—frequently (or usually) through my own actions— brings deeper faith and reliance upon Him. The struggles, and His intervention in the midst of them, adds quality to my character, and appreciation for His. But there is another verse that I am tying to use more, at the same time that I am trying to use Romans 8:28 less. That verse is Psalm 32:9.

> Do not be like the horse or the mule,
> which have no understanding but
> must be controlled by bit and bridle or
> they will not come to you.

You see, although I firmly believe Romans 8:28, and have put it to use time and time again, I am trying to gradually walk in alignment with Psalm 32:9 more, and to rely on Romans 8:28 less. Paul referred to the mechanism for switching from one level of Christian walk to another (better) method in 1 Corinthians 12. In it he is talking about spiritual gifts. And after some discourse he says something to the effect of, "But now, let me show you a *more excellent* way." What he is saying there is that the Corinthians were doing okay in a particular area of life ... but even so, there was a better, a more excellent way. And I have come to believe that there is a more excellent way of conducting my life than virtually *any* of the ways in which I currently conduct my life. I have come to believe that no matter how close I get to God ... no matter how lovingly and faithfully I may be serving Him or my fellow man ... no matter what lofty plain I may reach, there is a more excellent way. There is a way that is closer to Him ... a way that is more loving and faithful ... a place that is loftier. I want those ways.

I know I haven't mentioned the word *kairos* at all in this chapter, but bear with me. Going back to the verse about the horse or mule, which have to be controlled by bit and bridle. I believe with all my heart that if any person approaches God with an humble and honest heart, and asks God to direct his footsteps in this life, God will do it. It may be that He has to do it by harsh means (bit and bridle), but He will do it. But I believe there is a more excellent way. Otherwise, God wasted His efforts by putting a verse in the Bible that tells us to find that more excellent way. Jesus Himself told us about that way. Referring to Himself as the Shepherd in John 10:4 He says:

> When he has brought out all his own,
> he goes on ahead of them, and his
> sheep follow him because they know
> his voice.

So what does all of this have to do with kairos moments? This! Assuming that we have at least enough hunger for God to want Him to guide our lives, He has two means of accomplishing that. He can forcibly guide us, as with bit and bridle; or, we can learn to not only hear His voice, but to instantly obey what we hear, and to be guided by what we hear. I believe one of those means to be more excellent than the other. As pertaining to kairos moments in our lives

... they will come—and we will go through them. But did they accomplish the desired result as we came out the other side of them? Remember that kairos moments are the crossroads of life. They require decisions to be made, and those decisions are usually effected by whether or not we were prepared for the moment when it arrived. Jesus described one of the saddest events in His life in terms of the Jews' failure to properly recognize and respond to a kairos moment. Let's look at it. The event takes place late in His walk on Earth. He is approaching the city of Jerusalem riding on the donkey colt. We know it as the "triumphal entry."

> **As he approached Jerusalem and saw the city, he wept over it and said, "If you, even you, had only known on this day what would bring you peace—but now it is hidden from your eyes. The days will come upon you when your enemies will build an embankment against you and encircle you and hem you in on every side. They will dash you to the ground, you and the children within your walls. They will not leave one stone on another, because you did not recognize the time of God's coming to you."**
> **Lk 19:41-44**

Now you will notice the word *time* in the last sentence of that passage. In the English versions it is translated as time, but the word used was kairos. One of the few times that the Word mentioned Jesus weeping was on the occasion of the Jews, His people, failing to recognize the most significant kairos in the history of mankind. Did the fact that they were not prepared for the moment prevent the moment from arriving? No. It only meant that they failed to receive the benefit that could have been theirs if they had recognized it. It is the same way with us. God will bring us to the kairos' that He has planned for us. He will do it by bit and bridle if He has to. Or, He will do it by the more excellent way of speaking to us, and us obeying ... if we will allow Him to. But the important thing is this—the outcome of those kairos moments will be defined by how prepared we were for them when we got to them (or they got to us). If we are being directed to them by the force of bit and bridle, we are probably so busy being "forced" that we don't pay proper attention to where we are going. On the other hand, if we listen to His voice, He will talk to us along the way to those crossroads. He will give us some insights into what lies before us. He will begin to prepare us to make the proper responses and decisions. Then, when we get to those crossroads, unlike the Jews on that sad day, we recognize our kairos, whatever it may be, and navigate it in such a way that He rejoices rather than weeps.

I have talked at length about my belief in, and use of, Romans 8:28. I have also mentioned that I am trying to become less dependent on that verse, and to favor more excellent verses. That endeavor has caused me to face up to a truth in God's Word that I had never even thought about before. That is, not only is it *beneficial* for me to recognize kairos moments in my life so that I can make good decisions at my crossroads, but *it is actually expected of me.*

What would make me think that? Well, let me tell you. Have you ever thought about what Ephesians 5:16-17 means? It says:

> **"Be very careful, then, how you live—
> not as unwise but as wise, making the
> most of every opportunity, because
> the days are evil."**

What I quoted here is the NIV but in the KJV the word "opportunity" is translated "time," and the Greek word is kairos. We are commanded here to be careful how we live, and to make the most of every *opportune time* or kairos that comes our way. We are told to live as wise ones. Well, what is wisdom? I don't know the fullness of wisdom, but I do know that the beginning of wisdom is the fear of the Lord. So this verse could actually be translated, by comparing scripture with scripture, "As you go through these evil times in which you live, be on the lookout for kairos moments, and make the most of them. Live your life in the fear of the Lord, going carefully as you go." Notice that he said we are to make the most of every kairos. In order to make the most of them we must know that they exist and we must learn how to recognize them as we near them.

So, just how do we go about learning to recognize kairos moments? My first tendency would be to say, "Your guess is as good as mine." And it may be, because I am just beginning to learn about this myself. But I will tell you what I know, and hopefully it will turn out to be like so many of our high-tech inventions today. Alexander Graham Bell did not invent the cell phones that we all carry with us today. But he paved the way. He invented a very crude means of sending verbal communications over a wire. Well, others have come along since then and added their knowledge to his. They have applied their own creative ability to invent, to what he gave us, and it has evolved over time. Others will come along who have insights into the will and ways of God that I do not have and add to this discussion; and we may grow in our abilities to recognize kairos moments. But for starters, I think we have to rely heavily on the Holy Spirit to help us. John 16:13 says:

> **But when he, the Spirit of truth,**
> **comes, he will guide you into all truth.**
> **He will not speak on his own; he will**
> **speak only what he hears, and he will**
> **tell you what is yet to come.**

Now, does that mean that He will just tell us what is to come as far as the future of life here on Earth is concerned? Does it mean that He will only serve as a source of prophecy as we near the end? I do think it means that He will do those things. But I think it means more than that. I think that it means He will share with us on an individual basis, in general terms and sometimes in specific terms, what is to come in our own personal lives. I think it means that He is available to help us with recognizing a kairos when we near one. I think it means that He will also help us prepare to go through that kairos in the most beneficial way. Beneficial in what way? Beneficial both to His plans and purposes in the earth in this day, and also beneficial to us as individuals who are striving to find His plan for our lives ... and to live that plan out.

Do I think the verse means that He will only lead us into the truth hidden in the scriptures? Well, I certainly believe that there are truths hidden beneath the surface of the words in the Bible. And I certainly believe that the Holy Spirit waits eagerly to reveal the deeper things of God to those who will diligently search for them. But I believe it means more than that. I believe it means that He will lead us into truths that apply to us as individuals. Truths that may not even be written about in the Word. I don't mean that I think He will give us a revelation of new doctrine for the Christian faith. He has already provided all of that in the Scriptures. But there are things that you are going to encounter in the course of your daily walk that I am not going to encounter in mine, and vice versa. It would not have been appropriate to have addressed all of those individual things in the Word because you would have gotten so bored reading about my part that you might have set the Bible aside altogether. So He gave us Scripture regarding the parts that apply to all of us, and He sent the Holy Spirit to guide us into the truth of those things that apply to us as individuals.

How does He go about doing that? Well, to fully discuss that, we have to get into debatable doctrine (which is okay as long as we are not dogmatic). And I want to talk about both sides of this doctrine because both sides can be, and are, argued with scriptural backing. The nice thing about this particular discussion though is this. No matter which side of the debate you line up with, you still have the means, through the Holy Spirit, to recognize kairos times as they come your way. The debate comes in over the level of activity of the Holy Spirit in the believer's life today. The two sides, as you well know, are these. There are many who believe that the "baptism" of the Holy Spirit as it occurred in the second chapter of Acts is still available to believers today. And because of that, the gifts that He imparted in those days are still available and being imparted today. On the other side of the debate are the many who believe that that manifestation was for those days only and that the gifts that were imparted in those days passed out of usage with the death of the apostles. Those who align themselves with that side generally believe, to varying degrees, that the Holy Spirit, while not manifesting Himself in those particular ways any longer, is still available to teach us, and to guide us, and to comfort us, and to help us in numerous other ways. So no matter which way you believe, if you believe that the Holy Spirit has any activity in the life of the believer at all, you have access to Him for guiding you into the Truth as it applies to your life. And that would include showing you how to live according to the verse that I mentioned in Eph. 5:16, where He said to make the most of the kairos moments that come our way.

Now, because this topic has created so much division in the body of Christ, let me make a few side comments before we go on. Heaven is going to be filled with saints who spoke in tongues and operated in the Gifts of the Spirit on a regular basis, maybe a daily basis. It is also going to be filled with people who never prayed in tongues or prophesied once in their lives. Christ has welcomed both to be part of His Body and has not hinged that belief to salvation in any way. This book, this topic, and so much more of the plan of God for our lives is too important to have it dismissed over a disagreement of doctrine. Both groups will face kairos moments in their lives. Both groups have access to the Holy Spirit to help with those moments.

So which group should you belong to? That is not for me to say (certainly not in this book because that is not its topic). You need to be aware of the topic, and I believe we all need to do what I have done. I have gotten on my face before God and asked with a sincere heart what He would have me to believe. And I believe He has done that ... and my spirit is strongly established in that belief. Other people have done the same thing and yet believe the other side of the topic. What we each need to do is believe those things that Scripture plainly states are requirements of salvation. Beyond that, we need to tell God with a sincere heart that we want to walk this life with all of His Presence and direction that are available. And then, because everyone in both groups believes in the Holy Spirit, and the differences only come in what we believe to be His manifestations in this day, we need to ask Him to guide us into all truth. That is His job, and He is good at what He does. And having done that, and having applied faith to what we asked of Him, let it rest. If we ask with a sincere heart, He will guide each of us in the way we should go.

If we approach it in any other way, the strife and division that we have in our churches only grows and continues to separate the very body of Christ. It is way past time that we get beyond that and go on to maturity. Other than telling you those things that are a must for salvation, it is not my job to tell you what to believe. It is the job of the Holy Spirit. Remember, the Word said that *He* would lead us into all Truth. Does that mean we will all get at the absolute Truth at the same time? No. But if we believe those things essential for salvation, and earnestly seek the truth of the Word with open spirits, are we on the right path? Yes. Will the Holy Spirit come to the aid of the people in both groups? Yes. And will the divisions in the body of Christ begin to mend if we act in this way? Yes. Then, when the essentials of salvation bear fruit and we move on from this life, He will make sure that the absolute Truth is known to us ... and I suspect we will see how broken He was that we fought so vigorously over them among ourselves, all the while letting the lost tumble head over heels into Hell.

Having said that, and realizing that both groups

will benefit equally from learning how to handle kairos moments, let me talk for just a minute about how those in the second group might approach hearing from the Holy Spirit. You know the verse in Romans 10 that says " ... faith comes by hearing, and hearing by the word of God."(KJV) That is a wonderfully powerful verse if we ever get an understanding of it in our spirits. Well, right here is the opportunity for the Holy Spirit to do for us what He was sent to do. That is to guide us into the Truth. There are untold multitudes of scholars who have studied the scriptures from an academic point of view, and the Word of God never made any difference in their lives. It never brought even a little grain of faith to life within them. So the verse has to be more involved than to mean that faith will come any time we read the Word. And while we have to be careful not to exalt personal experience above the Word, I believe that there is wisdom in looking at the Word of God in light of our own experiences. This is what I have found as a general rule in my own life. I have found that a "once over" reading of the Word brings little, if any, change to my life. But if I read a verse and begin to meditate on it, letting it roll around in my mind and spirit, somewhere along the way that verse seems to come alive within me. It is as if the Word ceases to be something that was written to mankind in general, and becomes something that God has spoken into my spirit personally. The mechanism by which that happens is interesting, but is better saved for a future time. The important part is that the Word, in fact, seems to come alive inside me and becomes a personal thing. So, for instance, if I am sick, I ponder those verses that deal with God's provision for healing. If those verses are ever brought to life inside me, I know everything is going to be ok. I remember one time in particular that might serve as an example. It was at a time in my life when I was seeking God very diligently. I would get up very early every morning and spend about two hours in the Word and in prayer prior to beginning my daily routine. About that time I began to develop a nodule in the glands on my neck below each ear. I was tempted to have prayer for them but it was as if the Holy Spirit said to my spirit, "Wait!" So I did nothing. And I mean nothing. I didn't have anyone else pray for me and I didn't pray about the nodules myself. Meanwhile they continued to grow, and I began to be concerned, as did my wife—as by now they were each about the size of those baby carrots that we find on dip trays. Finally, one morning, as I was spending time in my prayer closet (which at that time was an actual empty closet), into my spirit came, "Okay, it's time to get rid of them. Lay your hands on your own neck and command the lumps to go." And it happened—not in the course of a few days or even minutes of time, but in an instant. The nodules collapsed under my fingers in what seemed like an absence of time. What I mean by that is that I could feel them and then suddenly, without perceiving them to be shrinking, I couldn't feel them. It is a little hard to describe. They never came back. I believe that was a kairos moment for me. I believe that if I had prayed earlier—before the opportune moment arrived—faith would have been absent, and only God knows what the outcome would have been. I believe that if I had waited until another time, I might have missed out, mostly because I would have been *afraid* that I had missed out through disobedience. Being afraid would have been a deterrent to faith. But by waiting for the Holy Spirit to bring the promise to life in my spirit, and by *immediately* doing what I believed He was telling me to do, it worked just like He said it would.

I believe it can work the same with the verse about the Holy Spirit guiding us into all Truth—including truth about all sorts of kairos moments that may be coming our way. So if I am sincere about wanting the Holy Spirit to help me see and prepare for those moments, I read that verse about Him guiding me into all Truth. And I search out other verses that speak of His leading me and guiding me and directing me. I begin to meditate on those and let them become part of me. As they do, faith rises in my heart. I begin to walk in a certain assurance that the Holy Spirit is involved in my life in a very dynamic way. I wake up expecting Him to be involved in my life each day. I walk with an expectation that He will show me opportune moments in my life—moments that can have an impact on the lives of people around me, or on the lives of my family members, or on my life. And it is a wonderfully reassuring thing to know that the Holy Spirit is playing an active part in my life.

So what about those who believe that the baptism of the Holy Spirit is still available today, along with speaking in tongues and the accompanying gifts that are listed in 1 Cor. 12 and 14. There is one particular part of that passage that I think becomes very relevant to seeking out and preparing for a kairos in our lives. It is the part that addresses speaking to God in tongues—in a "prayer language," as it is sometimes called. The verse is 1 Cor. 14:2.

> **For anyone who speaks in a tongue
> does not speak to men but to God.
> Indeed, no one understands him; he
> utters mysteries with his spirit.**

Take that verse and read it in conjunction with Rom. 8:26-27.

> **... We do not know what we ought to
> pray for, but the Spirit himself
> intecedes for us with groans that
> words cannot express.   And he who
> searches our hearts knows the mind of
> the Spirit, because the Spirit intecedes
> for the saints in accordance with
> God's will.**

The person who takes these verses into his spirit would seem to have somewhat of an easier path to take than the others. The reason is this. *Those who do not have* this teaching as part of their lives have a responsibility to actually find out what the kairos times of their lives consist of in order to prepare for them, and take advantage of them. *The people who do have* these verses as part of their daily lives have some of the responsibility taken from their shoulders and placed in the care of the Holy Spirit. For them, there may be a heaviness, or burden, that comes over their spirit—as others may experience as well—and they recognize it to be a burden to pray. But, in order to pray accurately, and therefore effectively, a person either needs to know the nature of the burden (as well as what God desires to see happen in that particular situation), or else be able to depend upon the Holy Spirit to intercede for them according to God's will. That can be done either by praying mysteries to God in an unknown tongue or else by having unintelligible groanings rise up from within their spirits. The Holy Spirit prays directly to the Father (intercedes) in their behalf. A person in that group can make preparations for a future kairos moment without ever knowing what that kairos involves until it arrives. The Spirit intercedes for her and helps pave the way toward the kairos, possibly without the details of the kairos ever having been actually revealed ahead of time.

But remember this. No matter which group you align yourself with, we are all part of the one and same body. The body of Christ. We each will face kairos moments in our lives and we each have access to the Holy Spirit for help in navigating those spots. And finally, remember that if we want God to guide us, He only has two ways to do so. One is by bit and bridle (force) and the other, more excellent, way is by hearing His voice and acting on it.

The word that Paul, to the Romans, wrote,
Has comforted me. And though I note,
That to me it has good things brought,
A more excellent way, in Him, I sought.
For to be raised up from a rubbish pile,
Is the lower way; and so while,
It is far better than remaining there,
To find that higher way, I think I'll dare.

Lord, if listening for You, I begin to stray,
Then with bit and bridle, make sure I stay
In the path with You—closely, so that as we walk
I will sense You there, and will hear You talk.
Show me those things that yet lie ahead,
Those kairos points, about which You have said,
"Crossroads are coming, and hard they will seem,
yet I will be there, if you let Me, your times to redeem."

CHAPTER 3

The Hindrance

So, if we see the importance of preparing for our kairos moments, and recognize that we would do well to enlist the help of the Holy Spirit to guide us through them successfully, why do we do so poorly at so many of them? How do we too frequently end up not doing what we should at the crisis moments of our Christian walk? In order to understand that, we need to have a clearer picture of what actually takes place at those crossroads. And whether or not we have ever thought about it, the Bible gives us a very clear picture of exactly what happens.

Have you ever thought about any of the various television commercials which portray a person in a quandary over what to do? On one shoulder sits a "haloed" angel and on the other sits a "pitchforked" devil. The angel is telling him the right thing to do and the devil is giving him other (usually more selfish) advice. They are comedic, cartoon-like representations, yet they are very descriptive of what the Bible portrays ... except for the halo and pitchfork. Let's look at those two characters that are sitting on our shoulders trying to influence our decisions. Ezekial 28:12-15 describes one of them in this way.

> " ... You were the model of perfection,
> full of wisdom and perfect in beauty
> ... every precious stone adorned you:
> ruby, topaz and emerald, chrysolite,
> onyx and jasper, sapphire, turquoise
> and beryl. Your settings and mount-
> ings were made of gold; on the day
> you were created they were prepared.
> You were anointed as a guardian
> cherub, for so I ordained you. You
> were on the holy mount of God; you
> walked among the fiery stones. You
> were blameless in your ways from the
> day you were created ..."

Have you ever thought about that passage in the Bible? What a beautiful description we are given of one of God's loveliest creations. And this isn't just a man talking about one of God's creations—it is God speaking through one of His prophets. He was saying, "Will you just look at that? That is the very best work I have ever done. It is absolutely perfect in form and function." What an accolade.

So, which "shoulder sitter" is God talking about here? To read it, you would think this was the "angel" giving good advice, but it isn't. If you have ever read this passage before, you will probably remember. This is God's description of Satan before he fell, or was cast down, from heaven. He was the very loftiest, the very wisest, the very most beautiful and the most powerful of all God's created beings. And now, he is the *mortal enemy of our souls.* This is the creature that we find ourselves pitted against at the crossroads of our lives. And just as God is eager for us to make good decisions at our kairos', Satan is eager to give us other advice. Let's examine him and how he goes about his task.

What did we read in that verse at the beginning of the quotation? We read that Satan was created *full of wisdom.* Did he lose that wisdom when he fell? Absolutely not! But his wisdom did change. The same verses that talk about his wisdom go on to say,

"... you corrupted your wisdom because of your splendor."

And we can see that the Bible still considered him to be wise after his fall because another verse tells us that we are to be as wise as serpents and as harmless as doves. Is this referring to physical, natural serpents like we have in our landscape today? Of course not. Satan possesses a spirit of wisdom, and he is the serpent. It is just that his wisdom has been corrupted and is not harmless. We are to desire to be wise, but not in a corrupted way. So as you go about your life, don't take lightly the wisdom of your mortal enemy. Do we walk in the wisdom that we should? If not, we are at an immediate disadvantage.

So, how does Wise Serpent use that corrupted wisdom to sway us? He has a variety of ways, but let me describe one of the primary ones. Since you are reading this you most likely believe that God is the "Big Boss." And by that, I mean that there is no one above Him in the chain of command. What He says, goes. Satan may seem large and overwhelming at times, but he is small in power and stature when compared with our Heavenly Father. Believing that, you would likely agree that to do what God would have us do would be wise ... or Wisdom, and to do what His sworn enemy would have us do would be foolish ... or Folly. And that is the area that Satan most often uses to try and sway us. He tries to get us to listen to his corrupted wisdom—Folly, instead of God's pure wisdom—Wisdom. And that is where the television commercial comes in. But instead of examining the commercials, let's look at how the Bible describes it.

Representing the "pitchforked" character we have Folly.

> The woman Folly is loud; she is
> undisciplined and without knowledge.
> She sits at the door of her house, on a
> seat at the highest point of the city,
> calling out to those who pass by,
> who go straight on their way. "Let all
> who are simple come in here!" she

says to those who lack judgment. **(Pr. 9:13-16)**

And representing the "haloed" character in
Pr. 8:1-4 and 9:3-4 we have Wisdom.

Does not wisdom call out? Does not
understanding raise her voice? On the
heights along the way, where the paths
meet, she takes her stand; beside the
gates leading into the city, at the
entrances, she cries aloud: "To you,
O men, I call out; I raise my voice
to all mankind.   ... she (Wisdom) calls
from the highest point of the city. "Let
all who are simple come in here!" she
says to those who lack judgment.

How do we put this to use in our daily life?
How do we relate God's *true* wisdom, Satan's
corrupted wisdom, and our *need for* wisdom to the
kairos moments in our lives?   Jesus told us that the
way, or path to the kingdom of heaven is straight and
narrow. So apparently Jesus compares this walk on
Earth to walking a path. The very first and most basic
method that Satan will use to destroy us is to tempt, or
trick us into leaving that narrow path. That path is his
first battlefield. He doesn't have to kill us. If he can
just keep us from finding the path, or, if having found
the path, he can get us to leave the path, he has won.
        The Holy Spirit, on the other hand (or shoulder)
is present to guide us into all Truth. How does that

process work? I mean, how do God and Satan come together to draw us to themselves along the paths of life? It is portrayed for us very clearly in the Proverb that we just cited. Let's look at it again and make a comparison between Folly and Wisdom. The Biblical description is more similar to the television commercials than you might think.

About Folly, Proverbs 9:3-4 says:

> The woman Folly ... sits at the door
> of her house, on a seat at the highest
> point of the city, calling out to
> those who pass by, who go straight
> on their way. "Let all who are simple
> come in here!" she says to those
> who lack judgment. (Pr. 9:13-16)

And about Wisdom it says:

> Does not wisdom call out? Does not
> understanding raise her voice? On
> the heights along the way, where
> the paths meet, she takes her stand;
> beside the gates leading into the city,
> at the entrances, she cries aloud:
> "To you, O men, I call out; I raise
> my voice to all mankind. (Pr. 8:1-4)

And then in 9:3,

> ... she (Wisdom) calls from the

highest point of the city. "Let
all who are simple come in here!"
she says to those who lack judgment. (Pr. 9:3)

First, let's look at the beckoning call of
Wisdom. The verse said, "On the heights along the
way, *where the paths* meet, she takes her stand; beside
the gates leading into the city, at the entrances, she cries
aloud: "To you, O men, I call out; I raise my voice to
all mankind." Think back to what we defined as a
kairos moment. It is a crossroad in our lives ... a place
where divergent paths meet ... a place where a decision
will have to be made. God has made sure that, at those
points, His wisdom, which is pure and uncorrupted, is
available to those who would have it.

Now let's look at the beckoning call of Folly
(and I like to look at Folly as being any thought or
action that is *contrary* to Wisdom). "The woman Folly
is loud; she is undisciplined and without knowledge.
She sits at the door of her house, on a seat at the highest
point of the city, calling out to those who pass by, who
go *straight* on their way." Does that sound like a
familiar scene? Of course it does. It is the same thing
that Wisdom is doing— positioning herself along the
paths of life calling out to those who go *straight* on
their way. Well, what kind of *way* are we on. We have
already said that *straight is the way* that we are to walk?
Well, if the way is straight and there are no crossroads
to confuse us, our walk is easy. But Satan sees to it that
that is not the case. He positions his corrupted wisdom,
Folly, at all of the crossroads where God has placed His

true wisdom, Wisdom. They both wait for us at those crossroads ... at those kairos', if you will. And when they see us coming, they both call out, "Come this way." It is a crossroad of life. It may only be a small one, or it might be the defining point of our life, but it is a crossroad none-the-less. When we get there we make our choice. And the choice we make determines what our next crossroad will be. If we choose Wisdom's pathway, the next kairos that we get to will likely provide an opportunity to go deeper with God—a place where we might discover things about Him that we never knew before. A place where He might allow us to do things for the Kingdom that we were never allowed to do before.

But what if, at that small crossroad, we chose the path of Folly? What if it was only something as small as "innocent flirting"? Well, it was a crossroad and we made a decision. We have to be on *some* road and possibly without even realizing it, we chose Folly's. It will lead us to our next crossroad, or kairos. But will it be the same crossroad, or kairos that we would have come to if we had chosen Wisdom rather than Folly? It *can't* be the same one because we are not on the same path that we would have been on if we had followed Wisdom's call.

So what happens if we go down that path? Well, Wise Serpent will see to it that we have another "opportunity" to be tempted. He is a master at it. And now he knows a weak area in our lives. We have already shown him that we have a propensity to make foolish decisions in a certain area of our life, and the

next crossroad will give us the opportunity to follow
him deeper. He may not be able to tempt you with
adultery today, but if he can get you to flirt today,
maybe he can get you to watch a lust-producing movie
tomorrow. And that might open the door for you to
enjoy some downright filthy websites that "inadver-
tently" popped up on your computer. Well, now your
wife finds out about that and she is wounded. She
becomes cold toward you because you have degraded
the loving intimacy that you had in your marriage.
Your relationship with her suffers and sexual frustration
sets in. And now you are set up. A woman with
perfectly innocent intentions comes along, or maybe
with no intentions at all. Maybe her path has been
similar to yours, or maybe not. Maybe she has just
come out of a bad relationship, or maybe not. Maybe
she is a friend for whom you have long had an attraction, but have resisted because of the strength of your
marriage; but now your marriage is weaker. The attraction, or the loneliness, or some other quality draws you
together. Now might you be in a position to consider
something that you would not have considered just a
few decisions ago? Maybe so. Why? Because you
came to a small kairos and chose the wrong path. That
led to another crossroad, and again you chose the
wrong path. There was a series of these and now your
marriage and spiritual welfare are on the line—and
Satan has found that *opportunity*. Could this have
happened if you had chosen Wisdom at the first crossroad? Probably not, because *we stray by degrees*. We
fail at a series of small kairos' until we get to a big

kairos, and then we are hard put to make the right decision. We meet with a major failure.

And does it have to be in the area of improper relationships? Well, that is a prime area in this day and in our culture, but it could be in any of a huge selection of temptations. It could be in the area of financial propriety, or honesty or unforgiveness or ... anything that is contrary to the ways of God. But the important thing to remember is that although Satan's wisdom may be corrupted, he is still wise. He searches and he probes until he finds a weak spot—a spot where he can get you to make that first wrong choice—a spot where he can get you to take that first small step down his path rather than God's. When that happens, he has the advantage.

Well, what happens if, not very far down that path, you realize that you made the wrong choice, and you regret it? You want back on the path that God wanted you on in the first place. Can you just jump back over to God's path? Maybe, *but probably not.* You see, once you make that first wrong decision, you can't undo it. You can't go back and "unflirt." Things can never be quite exactly the way they would have been if you had made the other choice in the first place.

Let me explain, but before I do, let me explain something else. I wrote the original sequence of events from the perspective of a man making poor decisions relative to his relationship with his wife and also his relationship with God. But that certainly does not have to be the way it occurs. Women flirt too. The gender of the offender is of no consequence. Feel free to plug your gender in anywhere it is appropriate and change the spouse to a husband if that fits your case. In fact, just to be fair to the female gender, let's pick the story up from the perspective of the woman that was flirted with. The man we mentioned made a pass—not really even a pass—just an overture in a flirtatious way. But he doesn't know what is going on in your life right now. He doesn't know that you are accustomed to that sort of friendly office play, and in times past, it would have been no big deal. It has always been part of your life, and you rarely give it much thought. I mean, even though you are getting to be mid-life, you are still attractive. And guys still flirt ... although it doesn't seem to occur as often as it did when you were younger. And now, ever since your last child was born, and you retained a little of the extra weight, you have caught yourself putting on that "look" more than you used to. You know—the one that says, "No, I'm not available. But if you flirt with me, or catch me in the right situation, I *might* wink back at you ... or pucker my lips at you ... or make some other innocently friendly gesture." You know, it is the look that women (or men) sometimes take on just to prove to themselves that if they *were* interested in someone, that *that* someone would be interested back. And now, what with the post child birth figure and a few crow's feet and everything (any or all of which may be real or imagined without effecting our story—and once again it can apply to either gender because guys age and change shape, too ... and for lesser reasons than childbirth), well, it's just a good feeling to know you still have it.

DECISIONS, DECISIONS, DECISIONS

Anyway, I'm not wanting to meddle, just be relevant. But for whatever reason he made a pass, probably just in jest, and you winked back ... just in jest. He made a bad decision because he is now headed down the path that we described above; and now you have made one, too. And this time something is different, maybe because you were feeling the *need* to be flirted with. Does it matter that he didn't know any of that? No, because something inside you changed this time. It never had before, and it is almost imperceptible. Could it be that it has something to do with the post-partum processes? Could it just be that age thing? Could it be because you are not as happy with your own looks and figure as you once were? Could it be because your husband has turned into a beer guzzling, ballgame watching couch potato who hasn't even noticed that your figure has changed a little? Or maybe your figure hasn't changed at all. Or maybe you look more trim than ever, but he seems not to notice. Yes, it could be any of those ... or none of them. But it is something. And you are glad that someone noticed you enough to flirt. And you go to work the next day, maybe not hoping, but wondering if it will happen again. Or did you hope just a little? No matter, Wise Serpent is patient. But it doesn't happen again that day, and you think about it. The next day you wear that top that is cut a little lower than most of them that you own. Oh, I know. It wasn't for him. You just wanted to look nice ... and you did ... and he noticed. The next day, as he approached you at the vending machine, instead of just calling your name, he touched your shoulder from behind and said hi.

There is no set series of events when something like this happens. And you are right; maybe it will go absolutely nowhere. And maybe none of this describes you at all. But there is something. *All of us have something.* It is not fun or easy to admit to, but there is always something. And whether it is this scenario or another, our lives plot their course based on each of those tiny little kairos moments that we face. In this case, nothing has happened. No sins have been committed. No marriage vows have been broken. But you have chosen to follow Folly at the intersection, rather than to follow Wisdom. And none of the moments that you encountered since has left you closer to God, or even the same distance from Him. Each has led you a little farther down the wrong path. That is all Satan wanted. He is patient. He just wants you to take a few steps down the wrong path ... for now.

But you are a Christian woman—maybe not as committed to following God as you have been at other times, but you still love Him and want His will for your life. And the Holy Spirit begins to raise red flags to warn you. And He begins to convict you in your spirit that you have not chosen well. He even shows you that you have not come to this point intentionally, but got here carelessly, by degrees. And now that you see it, you want it fixed ... sort of. If only this had been like the other times in life and you hadn't developed a little bit of feelings for this guy. It sure would have been easier if that were the case. But it's not the case. You have noticed these feelings—and now there is a struggle within yourself. You have seen the danger and you want to change paths and do the right thing. But now it is because you know it is the right thing, and not something that necessarily comes from your heart. That is what I meant when I said that you probably couldn't just jump back to where you should have been in the first place. It is much harder now that you have a little interest. And you can tell that he does too.

I have come to believe like John Bunyan in the 1600's (not Paul Bunyan, the woodsman, but John, the devoted lover of God). I hope you have read his classic book, *The Pilgrim's Progress*. If you have, you will understand better what I say here. In that most wonderful of books, Pilgrim and his traveling companion are headed toward Celestial City. They come to a place in the path that is hard to travel upon. They notice that right across the fence is a pleasant looking path that seems to run parallel to the path they are on. So they decide to walk that path instead, assuming it to go to the same place their path does. Well, it does run alongside for awhile, but then, by very small degrees, it turns away from the main road. The next thing they know, they are caught at Giant's Castle where they almost lose their lives. God helps them escape after much pain and struggle, but there is no way to get straight back to the main road from there. They eventually do get back, but only by returning to where they crossed the fence in the first place. Once they returned to the place where they got off track, they reversed their decision and followed the right path. But the time they wasted, and the suffering they endured from the poor decision could not be erased. And that is usually the case with us when we stray. God will usually take us back to that same crossroad and let us make the decision all over again about which way we will go. But the pain and misery and lost time cannot be reversed. Not to mention the fact that our poor decisions sometimes lead to death (i.e. drinking and driving), and no opportunity is found to correct the mistake.

Kairos moments, even the smallest, teenie-tiniest ones, are so important, because at each of them we choose a path ... a path that directs us a little closer to God ... or a little farther from Him. God knows how important they are and He stations Wisdom at each of them to guide us. Satan knows how important they are and he stations Folly at each one of them to misdirect us. We, as the ones actually travelling the paths of life, need to become more aware of them. We need to understand their importance in our walk with God. And we need to begin to look and listen at each of them to hear Wisdom as she helps guide us through them.

> **My son, if you accept my words and
> store up my commands within you,
> turning your ear to wisdom and applying
> your heart to understanding, and if you
> call out for insight and cry aloud for
> understanding, and if you look for it
> as for silver and search for it as for
> hidden treasure, then you will under-
> stand the fear of the LORD and find**

> the knowledge of God. For the LORD
> gives wisdom, and from his mouth
> come knowledge and understanding.
> (Pr. 2:1-6)

And when does Wisdom do these things for us—and where does Wisdom do these things for us? At those crossroads of life, both large and small, that we now have come to recognize as kairos moments.

CHAPTER 4

The Example

The smell of fresh bread drifting to the road from his house made Ananias hasten his steps a little. He had already caught the smell of roasting lamb grilling a hundred yards before this, so he knew she was fixing his favorites. "She must be ready to make up," he said under his breath. It didn't make any difference to him why she was fixing it; he was tired and hungry and glad to have the smell ... and the roast. And he was ready to make peace with her, but he wasn't ready to give up ... and he planned to tell her so—right after he ate.

As Ananias walked through the living room and into the kitchen, he saw that Sapphira wasn't there. Surely he hadn't been wrong. It had to be coming from his house. Then he saw her under the arbor out back. She was cooking at the outdoor oven. "This is even better than I thought." He hurried out the back to where she was cooking.

" Fira, I'm back." He watched her as she turned the meat on the grill. The angle of the sun shining through the trellis allowed him to see her form through her summer dress. Now his heart quickened as if to match his step.

He knew she heard him, but she didn't turn. When he was close enough he slipped his arm all the way around her middle until his hand was resting on her growing abdomen. He loved to feel the baby growing and couldn't wait until their first son was born. "Fira," he said gently. He drew her toward himself, and after the tiniest teasing hesitation she turned to face him. She gave him that look that had first made him notice her. Was it only a year and a half ago? It didn't seem possible. They had become such lovers, and friends—and soul mates in their short married life together. What a blessing of God to be married to the perfect mate. They both felt the same.

As they stood, wrapped in each other's arms, her head against his chest tightly enough to feel his heart beat, she knew they could work *anything* out. "Oh, Ananias, I am so sorry." And then for awhile neither of them spoke.

Her back was toward the earthen hearth and she couldn't see the roast, but he could. He loved Fira, and something about her being pregnant—well, anyway some thoughts passed through his mind, but that roast sure looked good. He could see the little drippings of fat flame up as they hit the coals. "tsss ... tsss ... tsss."

The sizzling sounds only made the smell richer. Making up could wait, but that roast couldn't. It was almost done. He relaxed his hold on her and she understood.

As she turned back to the grill, she asked softly, "Did you decide anything?"

He lied. "No, but I did find out something. I was hoping we could at least talk about it some more." "Why does she have to have this absolutely unreasonable dedication to God," he wondered to himself. "Or better yet, why did that land have to belong to her in the first place?" If it had been his, the decision would have been easy. But it wasn't. Her folks had given it to them when they got married. And he wasn't really in favor of getting rid of it at all. In fact, he was hoping to build a new house on it after the baby was born, but she wanted to donate it to the church. He had finally agreed to it. Well what else could he have done? After all, it wasn't his in the first place. But couldn't she sell it and just give part of it to the church. He hoped what he found out today would help sway her mind.

Ananias forked the roast onto a platter while she took the bread out of the clay oven, and they headed back into the house. He poured himself some wine but knew she would have water. That is all she had drunk since becoming pregnant. They held hands as they bowed their heads. Ananias gave thanks to God for His blessings in their lives.

"So what is it that you found out that makes you think we need to talk some more? You *know* what I think we ought to do. And if we give the money to the church, God will surely bless us for it. You know we can't outgive God. Even if He never did anything else for us the rest of our lives, we couldn't begin to give back enough to truly say 'thank you' for letting us see the truth about the Messiah." Sapphira was firm on her decision.

Ananias started in. "I went to Bethel today and learned something that might make us both happy. Ehud told me of someone there that might want to buy the land. I looked him up and we talked. You know Jonathan told us that the place was worth about 120 denarii. Well, this guy in Bethel—his name is Hadan—said he would give us 165 denarii for it. I know you want to give the money to the church, and so do I. I mean, if everyone else is selling land and sharing what they have, it won't look right for us not to give too. But how about if we give 120 denarii to the church, and keep 45 for ourselves? It's not like we would be cheating God or anything. The land is only worth 120 and that is all we should actually be getting for it anyway. If we sold it to someone around here that is all we would get. It might be that God sent this guy to us with a better offer just to bless us anyway. So why can't we just give the church what the land is worth and thank Him for blessing us with some extra?"

Sapphira listened. There had to be some common ground that they could come together on. Even God expected that. A marriage couldn't be all one-sided and be good for both people. Something about the plan still bothered her, but maybe he was right. Maybe she was a little too "straight-laced". She didn't answer, but she thought. Then she changed the subject. She had felt the baby move today. She seemed to almost glow as they finished dinner.

As they climbed into bed that evening Ananias brought up the subject again. "Well, what do you think? Fira, I just can't see how God could be mad at us for giving the church 120 denarii. I mean that's four months' wages for us. I bet everybody who has been selling their lands hasn't given every last denarius of it to the church. You can't tell me that God doesn't expect us to take care of our families. And He expects us to use wisdom with what He gives us."

"I know, but it just seems like lying to me ... I mean, to say that this is the money that we got for the land."

"We don't have to say that. We can just say that we sold some land and we want to give this money to the church," Ananias complained. "It's not like they are going to come right out and ask us if this is the exact total that we got."

"Well, I guess it wouldn't actually be lying if we did it that way, but it still bothers me." Sapphira raised her head up and gave Ananias a peck as she twisted her wavy hair to keep it from spreading all over her pillow, and Ananias' face. They both turned on their left sides and snuggled to start out, but soon Ananias was too hot. He turned his back toward hers and scooted over a bit. He never budged for the rest of the night.

Sapphira was different though. Something inside her was struggling ... and it wasn't the baby. Her spirit refused to rest, and it kept her tossing. Finally, just when she thought that surely it must be time to get up, she drifted off into a dream. In the dream, she saw her mom and dad. It was her dad's birthday. Her mother had sent her two goats to cook outside, the way her father liked them. She was to cook them and bring them to the house for a surprise. The two goats would be enough for all the children, and their children. As she dreamed, she saw the huge amount of meat that she had grilled and packed up to take to her folks. When they got there and everyone was preparing to eat, she opened the meat and there was only a morsel. Everyone just stood looking at her. Finally her mom broke the silence. "Sapphira, are these the goats I sent you?" And she woke up.

Later that morning, Ananias headed out. They both agreed that no matter what they did with the money, they ought to go ahead and sell the land while they had such a good offer. As he went, Ananias was happy over the compromise that he thought they would reach. Sapphira stayed home still worrying whether or not it was the right thing.

"I've got the money," were the first words that Fira heard when her husband came through the door early that afternoon. "And as part of the deal, I made the guy swear not to tell anyone what he paid us. But he was all to happy to agree to that because he knew he was paying a premium price for it."

"So the only people who have to know are the three of us," she asked?

"That's all. Well, there were the two witnesses

to the transaction, but they don't know us. They just witnessed it."

A short hour later Ananias was proudly standing before Peter and some of the other apostles. "We had some land that my wife's parents gave us. Since we weren't using the land yet, we wanted to sell it and give the money to the church to help take care of those that don't have money. Here is the 120 denarii."

Peter reached out gratefully to take the bag of money from Ananias' hand. As his fingers touched the pouch it was as though something wanted to erupt inside his chest. And while intending to say, "Thank you, Ananias," he felt different words rise up from deep within his spirit. "Is this the price you got for the land?"

Ananias was taken aback. He hadn't heard them ask anyone else that question. "Hurry up Ananias, you can't just stand here or they will know something is wrong," he said to himself. He decided they couldn't know what he had been paid ... not this quickly. "Yes, that is all it was worth." It didn't really seem like a lie because that *actually was* all that it was worth, but even before the words had cleared his lips he knew he had made a mistake; and a heaviness overwhelmed his spirit. He wanted to change his story, but how would that look now. He just couldn't do it.

And as Peter began to speak, Ananias began to quake in fear. He had barely heard the last of Peter's words when his heart just shut down and he fell to the ground.

When dinnertime came and Ananias still hadn't

come home, Sapphira went to where the apostles were taking the donations to see what had detained her husband. There was an awkward silence as she approached. "Hello Sapphira," Peter spoke up as she reached him. She was surprised that he knew her name. They had only talked one time. "Ananias came in today and gave us 120 denarii for the community fund. Is that how much you got for the land that your parents gave you?"

"I thought they weren't going to ask us that," she thought to herself, aggravated all over again for allowing Ananias to put her in this position. Peter gazed intently into her eyes as she continued trying to give an answer. She wanted to just tell the truth, but she also wanted to say the same thing Ananias had said so her husband wouldn't look foolish. She knew she needed to say something, so she made the decision. I will fudge the truth this one time, but never again. I hate this dishonesty. "Yes, that is the price...."

What I have written is obviously fiction. I took liberties with a true story from the Word of God. And I did it in a way that is almost angering. It may even cause some to put the book down because I have described things that a God of love would never do; He almost becomes the "bad guy." Forgive me for writing the story in this way, but I had a reason. It is not too hard for us to accept it when God strikes down Ananias, but please God, spare Sapphira. She loves you and is doing the best she can to serve you. She is young and lovely and delicate ... and carrying a baby, an innocent baby.

We only have a very short account of these actual events in the Bible, and we need to look at the *true* story before we go on. It is found in Acts 5.

> Now a man named Ananias, together with his wife Sapphira, also sold a piece of property. With his wife's full knowledge he kept back part of the money for himself, but brought the rest and put it at the apostles' feet. Then Peter said, "Ananias, how is it that Satan has so filled your heart that you have lied to the Holy Spirit and have kept for yourself some of the money you received for the land? Didn't it belong to you before it was sold? And after it was sold, wasn't the money at your disposal? What made you think of doing such a thing? You have not lied to men but to God." When Ananias heard this, he fell down and died. And great fear seized all who heard what had happened. Then the young men came forward, wrapped up his body, and carried him out and buried him. About three hours later his wife came in, not knowing what had happened. Peter

> asked her, "Tell me, is this the price
> you and Ananias got for the land?"
> "Yes," she said, "that is the price."
> Peter said to her, "How could you
> agree to test the Spirit of the Lord?
> Look! The feet of the men who
> buried your husband are at the
> door, and they will carry you out
> also." At that moment she fell down
> at his feet and died. Then the young
> men came in and, finding her dead,
> carried her out and buried her beside
> her husband. Great fear seized the
> whole church and all who heard
> about these events.

I need to address the last sentence first although it has nothing to do with kairos moments. If we are going to see an increasing presence of God in His church in these days, we need to pay more attention to the verse that admonishes us to "work out our own salvation *with fear and trembling.*" In our culture we have lost a reverential fear for the power and presence and holiness of God. God will not dwell in the presence of sin. That is probably because sin cannot dwell in the presence of His holiness. That only gives him two options. One, He can stay away with His manifest presence. Or, He can show up in our midst, at which point more events like the one described here would occur. Lest I neglect to mention it later in this book, let me encourage you now to begin to *make the decision* to walk in an ever-increasing reverence for the holiness of our God. He is the all loving God who gave His Son to make provision for the forgiveness of our sins. However, just because He made provision to cover those sins does not mean He is inclined to tolerate them in His presence.

Now, back to Ananias and Sapphira. I need to admit something. I had a life-changing encounter with God, through Jesus Christ, forty-five years ago. Although I've not been as dedicated as I would like for all of those years, I have read this story many, many times. My opinion of Ananias and Sapphira has remained virtually unchanged for all those years—and that opinion has not been good. And it is still not good, *but it is different* since I have begun to examine this topic of kairos decisions. What I mean is this. God did not tolerate their behavior, and so I can't either ... but I do have a better understanding of it. And even though I believe I now have a clearer picture of how this could have happened, it still scares me because I see things in my life that are as bad as what was in theirs. I hope that Ananias and Sapphira were not at all like I described them. I hope they were older and wealthy and the selling of the land was just for show—and had no impact on their finances whatsoever. But that might not have been the case. They could have been anyone ... in any station of life. I suspect that they did not get into trouble in the way I described it, but they got there somehow, and I don't believe it was because they were evil people.

Let's talk about the scenario as it existed in that

time. The church was in its infancy. Jesus had been crucified and had ascended into Heaven. He had sent the Holy Spirit to empower the believers. Miracles were being performed by the apostles and others on a daily basis, and on a grand scale ... and people were coming to Christ—by the thousands. Sometimes they were coming by the thousands per day. There was no New Testament available to give all those converts guidance. There were not a lot of spiritual overseers to help the believers mature. Some were coming out of a pure adoration and appreciation for Jesus Christ. Others were joining because it was the "thing to do." But what about Ananias and Sapphira? We don't know the answer to that.

So, what makes my heart break for them? What makes me think that there could have been circumstances present that would help explain their actions? One thing! And if it weren't for that one thing, I could just read right through this story saying, "They got what they deserved," and gone on with my reading. And before I go on at all, let me say that they did in fact get what they deserved, because God is the righteous judge and He determined that it was just. But even though it was just, it wasn't necessary, and it could have been avoided, maybe by reading this book.

Anyway, this one thing makes me hurt for them; and it makes me wonder how they came to do what they did. That one thing is in the very first verse of the story. Notice that it said that Ananias and Sapphira sold some of their own land and brought at least a substantial part of the money to the church to help support those that did not have means to support themselves. All my life I have been critical of them for not bringing all of the money. All my life, I have read God's viewpoint of the event and judged them with His judgment, all the while falling short myself. You see, I have spent my life trying to have enough money to buy a little land and to use what I have to provide for my family to the best of my ability. Here were Ananias and Sapphira who owned a piece of land. They did not hesitate to sell it and bring most of it to put into the church treasuries. *I have never done that, and neither have most of the people who will read this book.* God could never strike me down for lying about how much I got for the land, because I never gave it to God in the first place. There was something in Ananias and Sapphira that was more noble, or more dedicated, or more something, than there is in me. And that makes me want to dig deeper and find out what went wrong.

That is where the little story at the beginning of this chapter came from. It was just me pondering (I warned you about me doing that) how it could have happened. I am reading about a man and a woman who were birthed into the body of Christ in its earliest stages. They are willing to give up a chunk of their possessions for the cause of Christ, and yet they both ended up dead prematurely. I hope they weren't a lovely young pregnant couple, but they could have been. They could have been anyone. They could have been me ... or you. I know this is a hard chapter, but if we are ever going to go on to maturity, we have to begin to look at things like this. And then we have to fix them with the help of the Holy Spirit. God isn't interested in going around striking believers down. What He *is* interested in is having a bride to present to His Son ... a bride who is holy and blameless, without stain or wrinkle. You might ask, "Well, doesn't the blood of Christ make us holy?" Indeed, we are cleansed by His blood, but there is more to being a holy bride than being covered by His blood. We are told in 1st Peter to be holy *in all that we do*. That is a command to us. It is not the holiness that comes through His blood; it is something He expects us to *do*. It was something He expected Ananias and Sapphira to do. And as we get near the end of this chapter, we finally get to the topic of this book. We avoid the Ananias and Sapphira situations by paying attention to the kairos moments in our lives. We perform the act of "being holy in all that we do" by making proper decisions at the kairos' of our lives. We stay on the way that is narrow and straight by choosing the right path at those crossroads of life.

You see, if you are a person who is inclined to sell your land and give the money to the church, you are not just going to get up one morning and agree with your spouse to lie to the Holy Spirit. Remember what I said earlier. We stray by degrees, sometimes very small degrees. I don't believe Ananias and Sapphira were any different. I believe they made a true start. I believe they were sincere in their walk with God. But somewhere along the way, Wise Serpent saw a chink in their armor. He saw a weakness that he could exploit. Was it in Ananias? We don't know. Was it in a delicate and lovely Sapphira? We don't know. Did they both wander off in a way that would cause them to be less than honest before the throne of God? We don't know. But we can be fairly sure that if they had been evil through and through, they never would have become associated with the Christian sect in the first place. They would have had to undergo some ridicule and criticism to become a believer in "The Way." They would have been considered traitors to Judaism ... heretics.

So I have to believe that they started out in sincerity, just as we have. I have to believe they had a love for God and the Son He sent, just as we do. But I believe that when they arrived at their crossroads, they made a series of poor decisions ... just as we can. This went on until they reached the point that at least one of them, probably Ananias, cared more about the approval of man than he did the approval of God. Do I have a scriptural basis for this position? Yes, one that comes from *thinking* about the words rather than just reading through them. I suspect it was Ananias rather than Sapphira because the Word says that he did it. It doesn't say Sapphira approved of it or did it, just that she had full knowledge of it. And as to why I believe that they had started off on the right track, Peter asked Ananias, "How is it that Satan has so filled your heart that you have lied to the Holy Spirit ... ?" You see, Peter was surprised at what happened. He knew that at one point in their life, this was not a decision that they would have been likely to make. He wanted to know what went wrong. What happened that allowed them to get to this failure at a major kairos in their lives. And what happened was that before they failed at this huge crossroad, they failed at a series of smaller ones.

No matter what their social status or their financial level, the real Ananias and Sapphira failed at the crucial crossroads in the same way that the imaginary people earlier in the chapter did. They failed at their major crossroads in the same way that I have failed in my life, and that you probably have in yours. Their failure came about in the same way that virtually every failure has *ever* come about. That is by failing to recognize small crossroads for what they are—the determiners of our destiny. They are the points that set us on paths. Every path leads to somewhere ... either toward a closer walk with God, or in a direction farther from Him.

So far I have only talked about those decisions that led people into trouble in their lives. I guess that is appropriate because that is where I have spent most of my life. Rarely intentionally, but on the wrong path none-the-less. I have been exactly like the people that Jesus described when He wept over Jerusalem. I have all too often failed to recognize the time of God's kairos moments in my life. Now that I look back, I believe, and hope, that it is because I didn't understand about kairos' at the time. I didn't understand what a special and precious thing the larger of those times could be. And because I didn't know about the importance of the large ones, I failed to prepare for them at the smaller crossroads.

God, please help me to see that my
final destiny is determined at the
significant kairos crossroads of my life.
Help me to understand that I prepare to
recognize and successfully navigate
those large crossroads by paying attention to the tiny ones that come my way
every day of my life. Give me the
wisdom, Oh God, to choose the right
path *every single time* that I come to a
place where there is a path to choose.

Amen

CHAPTER 5

Explanations and Angles

Ananias and Sapphira are dead ... struck down in the presence of God. And what was their sin? It was called lying to God. But what did it consist of? Was it that they only brought part of the money that they got from the land that they sold? No. They didn't have to bring any money at all. In fact, if they had not brought any money at all they probably would have lived out their lives. What if God had spoken to their spirits and told them to sell the land and bring the money, and they refused? Although the blessing of God would likely have been lifted from them, and their finances might have been hindered, they probably would have lived out their lives. They would have failed that particular kairos by choosing not to be obedient, in which case the path they chose would have led them to another cross-road. But it is not likely that they would have died on the spot. Otherwise, I would not be alive to write this, and you would not likely be alive to read it, because we have all been disobedient.

So, what was their sin? Let's consider two scenarios. In both of them they bring the same amount to the apostles ... let's say 120 denarii. In one scenario they bring the money and say that it was the total that they got for the land. In this scenario we don't have to imagine what would have happened because that is what they actually did (except that the amount is a made up figure). But what if, instead of saying that that was all that they got for the land, they took their money to the church and said, "Peter, we sold a piece of land. We got a really good price for it ... 165 denarii. We want to give a hundred-twenty of it to the church for the needy, but we are keeping forty-five for ourselves. What would have occurred as they presented it to the elders? They would have been *blessed* for their giving. And so, even though they gave the same amount in both scenarios, one way resulted in blessing and the other in death. What made the difference? Throughout the Bible you will find that it is almost never the act itself that God looks at, but rather the attitude of the heart. That is why God cautions us to:

> **"above all else, guard your heart, for it**
> **is the wellspring of life." (Pr. 4:23)**

Something in the heart of Ananias and Sapphira allowed them to lie in the presence of God. And I believe it was something they allowed to grow there. I believe that either one of two thoughts passed through their minds at that crossroad where they made their fatal mistake. Either they were filled with pride or they were filled with unbelief. Pride being the pursuit of the accolades of men. And unbelief being afraid that God might not take care of them if they gave away all the money from the sale of their "safety net." Pride is a sin. Unbelief is a sin. God didn't want either sin in His church and He took immediate steps to end it. And as a side note totally unrelated to our topic—He still doesn't want it in His church. And as He begins to manifest His presence in a greater way, I believe there will be more incidents of this nature. He will show us what type of behavior is required for the arrival of His manifest presence.

But back to our topic. If they were filled with unbelief (not believing in His willingness or ability to take care of their needs) they weren't the first to be corrected for that. Look at the pain and suffering that the Israelites went through after they came out of Egypt. They failed to enter into the Promised Land because of unbelief. They wandered in that desert wasteland for forty years because of unbelief. Every last adult except for two rested in sandy desert graves because of unbelief. Did Ananias and Sapphira find an early grave through unbelief? We don't know, but they could have. With unbelief (or without faith) it is impossible to please God.

Maybe it wasn't unbelief. Maybe it was pride. And that is the way the story sounds to me. It sounds as if they had wanted to make a show of their giving so that they could enjoy hearing people talk about the good deed they did. That is the pride of life. And pride is the very first recorded sin that brought the judgment of God. It wasn't in the life of a man, but of an angel. That was Satan's offence. He was cast from heaven and doomed to eternal destruction because he lifted himself up in pride. God cast him down because of his pride, and it may have been the same with Ananias and Sapphira. But whatever it was, it came about after a good and true start in the Christian faith. They failed at a series of small crossroads and then were not able to correct themselves when they got to a major crossroad. We must always remember ... we stray by degrees. And every tiny crossroad that we come to will either angle us toward God by a few degrees, or away from Him by a few degrees.

I know that the statement I am about to make may seem an oversimplification. It may be more than obvious to everyone who reads this book. And looking back at it, it almost sounds insulting to make a statement like this because it is plainly evident, and should not need stating at all. But the truth is, until I really began to ponder this topic in earnest, I had never really thought about what I am going to say. And that statement is this. Except for those events that have come into our lives through other peoples actions, every last soul among us came to be where we are by means of the decisions we made earlier in our lives. Oh, I know we have all thought about someone in prison, or someone with AIDS, or a drug addict on the streets, or a compulsive gambler who lost her family, or any one of many very sad situations, and we have said, "Well, they just made some really bad decisions, and this is where they have ended up." And before I go on, let me say that I know that not everyone in prison or with AIDS or on drugs got there out of bad choices that they made. There are people wrongfully imprisoned. There are children with AIDS infected by parents. There are parents infected by incidental blood contact. One spouse may have become infected through the infidelity of the other spouse. There are people addicted to drugs who became that way after a painful accident. But for the most part, those maladies come to pass by poor decisions. But when I say that each of us got here through the decisions we have made, those disasters are not even the type of thing I am talking about. Most of the people reading this book do not find themselves in any of those situations. This book isn't written to the lost. It is not written to try to bring souls into the kingdom of God. It isn't even written to the nominal Christian. It is written to those children of God who subscribe to the Army slogan ... "Be all you can be." There is a group of people rising up who want to *be* more, and *do* more in the kingdom of God than they ever have before. They are a people who want to see their King assume His position as Ruler of Earth. They do not want to build their own kingdom; they are trying to increase the glory of His kingdom. They do not want positions or titles; they want Him. They are not deluded into thinking they can *do things* to pay Him back for what He has done for them, but *they want to see if there are at least things they can do to say "thank you"* for what He has done. They do not want to be exalted, but they long to see Him exalted. They want to mature. They are His bride and want to be without spot or wrinkle or any such blemish. These people have an unquenchable desire to get just a little closer to Him, and when they do, they want to get yet a little closer. My parents are such people, and they surround themselves with such people. My spiritual heritage from them has made it almost impossible for me to escape that desire in my own life. My brothers are infected with it ... and it is wonderful—and wondrous. I am drawn to others who are that way. It is this type of person to whom this book is written. I believe you are one of these people, otherwise you have already given up on this book.

So, you see, this book is not really written to encourage you to avoid those decisions that will lead to the sad situations that I described earlier. It is much more subtle than that. It is written to help us see that it is the little crossroads or forks in the road that we face in life that determine our destiny. That is, in part, because they determine the paths of our day to day lives, and also partly because they influence which large crossroads we will come to, and how we will respond when we come to them. If you don't believe me, just ask Ananias and Sapphira.

Or, we can look at some other Bible characters and see if what I said was true in their lives as well. But first lets make some distinctions. My favorite all time television program is "The Andy Griffith Show." I know all of its black and white episodes by heart (possibly because of some poor decisions regarding priorities earlier in my life—but I could have done worse). But in that series we meet Otis, the town drunk. Now there are other people in the town of Mayberry who get drunk from time to time. But are they portrayed as the town drunk? No. Is any person who has ever gotten drunk, a drunkard? No, but rather it is the one who lives the "Otis" lifestyle who is a drunkard. I have, and you have, told a lie somewhere along life's way. Does that make you, or me, a liar? I don't think so. But there are those people who live a lifestyle of lying. The late humorist and wonderful storyteller, Jerry Clower, had a term for a person like that. He called them someone "who would climb a tree to get to tell a lie when they could have stood on the ground and told the truth." In other words, they seem to go out of their way to tell a lie. That person has no regard for the truth. They are a liar. The book of Revelation says that all liars will find their place in the lake of fire. That can't mean anyone who ever told a lie or else everyone except Christ would be in hell. It can only mean that person who lives a lifestyle of lying.

And the principle involved here is what I want to establish before we look at some other characters in the Bible. What we have said about drunkards and liars doesn't just apply to those two qualities or lifestyles. It applies to every form of lifestyle. We aren't gluttons because we over-eat on Thanksgiving—I guess that one is fresh on my mind because yesterday was Thanksgiving ... and, well. To move on though, the Proverb that talks about a little sleep, a little slumber, does not refer to someone who is tired from a week of work and catches a Sunday afternoon nap. It is referring to that person whose poverty has come about because they refuse to get up out of the bed and work. But the principle works on the other side of the coin, too. Someone who entertains a brief pursuit of God is not a "God Chaser." And the reason I put that in quotations is because of the excellent instruction that we can get from the books by Tommy Tenney. I can't think of that term without thinking of him and his book by that title. And I will talk more about his work and his books later in this book. But this whole discussion supports what I am saying. He has so been identified with pursuing the presence of God, that I can't say *God Chaser* without thinking of him. *Tommy Tenney is a God Chaser.* I can't think of a soul winner without thinking of Billy Graham. He has lived a lifestyle of bringing souls into the kingdom of God. I can't think of the term "intercessor" without thinking of my parents and other family members. That is what they are ... not because they intercede in a crisis, but because that is how they live. And with that in mind, let's look at the lives of a few Bible characters.

There was a seldom-mentioned man in the Old Testament that was so consistent in his behavior that he earned a descriptive title (much like Otis did in the Andy Griffith Show). The Bible said he was surly and mean in his dealings. It wasn't just that he was that way on the occasion being written about, but that was his lifestyle. His name was Nabal, the husband of Abigail. Abigail, on the other hand, while not having

been titled, displayed a totally different set of personality traits. Let's look at them. The scene takes place
while David is in a wilderness area after having fled
from King Saul. David had a band of men with him.
Now you have to remember that there were not police
departments and other law enforcement agencies in
those days. People in remote areas were left to defend
their own families and property. Part of what David did
while in that area was to help keep raiders and thieves
from taking the property of the residents around him.
He had done that for Nabal and Abigail. The Word
says:

> "While David was in the desert, he
> heard that Nabal was shearing sheep.
> So he sent ten young men and said to
> them, "Go up to Nabal at Carmel
> and greet him in my name. Say to
> him: 'Long life to you! Good health to
> you and your household! And good
> health to all that is yours! "'Now I
> hear that it is sheep-shearing time.
> When your shepherds were with us,
> we did not mistreat them, and the
> whole time they were at Carmel
> nothing of theirs was missing. Ask
> your own servants and they will tell
> you. Therefore be favorable toward
> my young men, since we come at a
> festive time. Please give your servants
> and your son David whatever you can

find for them.'" (1 Sam. 25:4-8)

What is happening is this. David is sending messengers to say, "Hey, look, my men and I are out here in the desert. We are strong enough that we could have taken everything that you own. But we didn't. And not only did we not take your stuff, we didn't allow raiders to come and take your stuff. We were kind to your herders. We have been a good neighbor. But, we don't have lands or herds of our own. Since we have been good to you, would you consider sending a few head of your livestock as payment for what we have done for you?"

But Nabal, probably from being puffed up at his wealth, and probably from believing that it was his harsh dealings that had gotten him to where he was, sent this reply back to David.

> **Nabal answered David's servants, "Who is this David? Who is this son of Jesse? Many servants are breaking away from their masters these days. Why should I take my bread and water, and the meat I have slaugh- tered for my shearers, and give it to men coming from who knows where?" (1 Sam 25:10)**

Little did Nabal realize it, but this was a kairos in his life. He had grown so accustomed to responding harshly that he never even considered the wisdom or foolishness of his answer. Maybe in his earlier days he was less surly and mean. We rarely are born that way, but rather we become that way over time. Maybe he even had a good reason for being that way. It may have been that in that harsh environment, putting on a harsh demeanor was the only way to keep from being swallowed up by stronger neighbors. But however he came to be that way, by the time he had his encounter with David, he had ceased to make any pretense of making wise decisions, and answered in accordance with his character ... surly. And in so doing, he failed a major kairos without ever knowing he was facing one. Look at David's response.

> **"David said to his men, "Put on your swords!" So they put on their swords, and David put on his. About four hundred men went up with David, while two hundred stayed with the supplies." (1 Sam. 25:13)**

Now it was at this point that *David* made a poor decision. He decided that he would kill every male belonging to the household of Nabal. It is true that Nabal may have deserved it, but God had told them, even back in those days, that vengeance was His job and that they were to let Him repay those who did evil. None-the-less, David and his small army headed out for Nabal's ranch.

Now Nabal's wife was not at all like him. She had developed a lifestyle of acting prudently. Look at

her first response when the servants told her what was
going on between her husband and David.

> "One of the servants told Nabal's
> wife Abigail: "David sent messengers
> from the desert to give our master his
> greetings, but he hurled insults at
> them. Yet these men were very good
> to us. They did not mistreat us, and
> the whole time we were out in the
> fields near them nothing was missing.
> Night and day they were a wall
> around us all the time we were
> herding our sheep near them. Now
> think it over and see what you can
> do, because disaster is hanging over
> our master and his whole household.
> He is such a wicked man that no one
> can talk to him." Abigail lost no
> time. She took two hundred loaves of
> bread, two skins of wine, five dressed
> sheep, five seahs of roasted grain, a
> hundred cakes of raisins and two
> hundred cakes of pressed figs, and
> loaded them on donkeys. Then she
> told her servants, "Go on ahead; I'll
> follow you." But she did not tell her
> husband Nabal." (1 Sam. 25:14-19)

Abigail did two things here that showed
wisdom in a kairos moment. First she sent a gift of

appeasement to the one that was coming to destroy her home and family. And secondly, she didn't tell her husband, who would have almost certainly thwarted her plans if he had known about them. A prudent wife.

Now I won't tell the whole story here, but it is a wonderful story and you need to read it for yourself. But the short of it is this. Abigail approached David with her gift as he was approaching her home to destroy it. In 1 Sam. 25:32-35 when he saw the gift she brought, and heard the petition with which she pleaded for her family, he said this.

> **"David said to Abigail, "Praise be to the LORD, the God of Israel, who has sent you today to meet me. May you be blessed for your good judgment and for keeping me from bloodshed this day and from avenging myself with my own hands. Otherwise, as surely as the LORD, the God of Israel, lives, who has kept me from harming you, if you had not come quickly to meet me, not one male belonging to Nabal would have been left alive by daybreak." Then David accepted from her hand what she had brought him and said, "Go home in peace. I have heard your words and granted your request."**

Now there are two important elements to what he said. First he said, "may you be blessed for your *good judgment.*" Abigail's' character stood out. The quality of making good judgments took over, and just as Nabal's character had caused him to act foolishly, Abigail's character caused her to act wisely. He failed his kairos moment without ever thinking about it, and she passed hers without ever having to think about it. Both of them came to a kairos moment and both made decisions that were influenced by the smaller decisions they had made earlier in life ... the one foolish and the other wise. But the important point is that this was not the first time either of them had acted foolishly or wisely. They had developed those characteristics over time at other smaller kairos moments—moments that defined this large kairos in each of their lives.

And the other thing of note here is that David said thank you to Abigail. Did you notice that as he was commending her for her good judgment, he was doing so because it kept him from taking vengeance with his own hands? Her good judgment kept David from acting on his own bad judgment.

Well, that is the end of the story as far as kairos is concerned, but I hate to leave the story unfinished. When Nabal heard what had gone on, he had a heart attack and died about ten days later. David sent messengers to ask Abigail to be his wife. She accepted and lived happily ever after ... more or less. But her decision at a major kairos spared her life and that of her household, while her husband's decision at that very same kairos cost him his life and almost that of his household. And both of them came into that kairos with character traits and mindsets that were determined at smaller kairos' long before they came to that major one.

So what we have to ask ourselves in order to make the story relevant to our own lives is this. Did Nabal have to be a surly, mean person, and did Abigail have to be a wise and prudent wife? I mean, even if they were born with natural tendencies to be that way, did they have to remain that way, or could they have changed the way they were? Can anyone change her character traits? Or, to make it a little more relevant to those of us reading this book, can a *born again Christian* change her personality traits? And when I ask that, I mean can she, by any means, change herself? That would include changing herself with the help of the Holy Spirit.

For instance, what if a woman had gone through life with no regard whatsoever for the truth—a woman of the type we discussed in the Clower stories. Now that lady comes to Christ. Is the tendency she had to lie, immediately taken from her? Possibly, but more likely she will still have that tendency, only now she will be convicted of the Holy Spirit when she yields to it. But, does God expect her to quit being a habitual liar? Absolutely! What does Revelation 21:8 say? It says that all liars will have their place in the lake of fire. Now we have already talked about who that does and does not mean. It doesn't mean that anyone who has ever told a lie will be in the lake of fire, else all of us would be there. Yet it says *all* liars will be there. And who did we define as a liar ... someone who lives a lifestyle of lying. Someone who has no regard for the truth—Mr. Clower's "tree climbing liar," if you will. Remember that the Word says that if we confess our sins, God is faithful and just to forgive us our sins. But from our heart we have to turn away from lying and strive to walk in a way that is pleasing to Him. It isn't the person who tells a lie that goes to hell. It is the person who doesn't hate lying and who doesn't turn from lying in their heart. That person hasn't made Christ Lord of their life. So, to answer our question, God expects us to quit being liars. If we can do it by a decision on our own, fine. If we have to call on Him for daily help, fine. But either way, we have to do it. The woman we are talking about has to begin changing the character trait of lying. She has to begin changing who she is.

Okay, let's talk about a married man who has repeatedly been unfaithful to his wife. Although his wife is a Christian, he wants nothing to do with God. She chooses to remain in the marriage and pray for her husband. Finally, one day he turns to God. Will the appetite that he had for extramarital relationships just vanish from his life? Maybe, but probably not. It will likely be the same for him as it was for the liar we just described. He will have an awareness through the Holy Spirit that not only is adultery a sin against his wife, but against his relationship with God. He will likely be tempted by Wise Serpent and face a kairos in that area of his life. If he fails, he will be convicted by the Holy Spirit, and will face another kairos. This kairos will be whether to fight the temptation with God's help, or just to give in ... which will lead to yet another kairos. But the point is that God will expect him to begin to hate adultery from his heart and to make an effort to cease his infidelity. God will forgive him if he fails, but he has to enlist the help of the Holy Spirit and continue to try.

And so it is with any character trait that you can name. If ungodly attributes are part of our lives, we have to begin to weed them out. If there is a lack of Godly attributes in our lives, we have to begin to cultivate them. Most of the ungodly ones are mentioned in the Bible and are labeled as sins. The Godly traits are essentially the things listed as fruits of the Spirit. The Word says in Gal. 5:22-24:

> **But the fruit of the Spirit is love, joy, peace, patience, kindness, goodness, faithfulness, gentleness and self-control. Against such things there is no law. Those who belong to Christ Jesus have crucified the sinful nature with its passions and desires.**

Anything that is contrary to any of these is something that needs to be changed in our lives. In Eph. 5:9-10, where it also talks about Christian fruit it says:

> **(For the fruit of light consists in all goodness, righteousness and truth) and find out what pleases the Lord.**

And then in another place, the Word says that if we want to fulfill the entire will and desire of God in our lives, we can narrow it down to just two points. We are to love the Lord our God with all our heart, soul, mind and strength, and we are to love our neighbor as ourselves.

If there is anything in your life that puts you in a position of loving the Lord your God less than "heart, soul, mind and strength," there is something in your life that needs changing. It may not be something that sends you to Hell, but remember, we have gone beyond the doctrine of salvation and of Heaven and Hell. We are trying to go on to maturity. We are trying to discover those things that allow us to draw ever closer to God, and to have an increasingly intimate relationship with Him. You see, God the Father and Jesus love all of us very much, but there is a more intimate place in God that I want to get to. It is even beyond the place that Mary and Martha and Lazarus found. And He loved them very much. It is beyond the intimacy that Jesus had with John the Beloved, and Jesus loved him enough to confide in him—and to give him the Book of the Revelation. I want to be closer to Him than Enoch or Elijah was. If I had to pick a level of relationship with God that I imagine to be perfect, it would be that of God and Adam. Do I think I can get that close to Him? Probably not ... but I can get as close as I can get. And I believe that there is a closeness that I have never even imagined yet. And I believe it can be attained while still on this Earth and in this body.

I think I have always believed that a close

personal relationship with God was possible, and I have even pursued such a relationship in a clumsy way at times in my life. But there is a scripture that describes my attempts. The verse is in Romans 10:2 where it talks about people having a zeal for God, but that their zeal was not based on knowledge. In fact, Paul himself fit nicely into that description before his "Damascus Road" experience. He had a great zeal for God, but he used that zeal to persecute and kill Christians. But as I have begun to see the truth about kairos moments, and have begun to tie that truth with revelation from other servants of God, I have a renewed interest and determination to bring intimacy to my relationship with God.

Let me explain. Every time I have read the book of Genesis in the past, a jealousy of sorts rose up inside me. The first thing I saw was that God was involved in Adam's day to day life in a very caring and ordinary, yet special way. Adam didn't come to God and say, "I need a partner." God was close enough to Adam that He noticed it on His own and provided for him. Adam didn't say, "God, it sure would be nice to have a garden and animals here to make life pleasant." God anticipated his needs and provided for them without Adam ever asking. Something like that does not occur without the existence of an intimate relationship between the two of them. And then, to top it all off, it seems as though God made it a habit of coming down to that garden "in the cool of the day" and hanging out with Adam. The only account we have of it doesn't actually say that, but it can be inferred. If you notice, Adam and Eve weren't surprised to hear God walking about amongst the trees of the garden; they were just ashamed because, for the first time, they realized they were naked. That nakedness (or actually the sin that made them aware of it) alienated them from the presence of God. But before that separation took place, there was quality, intimate time spent between Adam and God. And I will admit that I am jealous of that. And if that is the sort of jealousy that God declares to be a sin (and of course it is not), then I sin that very same sin every day of my life. And not only that, but I am more jealous of that intimate relationship with every single day that passes.

Well, knowledge that I have gained from the books that I mentioned earlier (and will mention again), and knowledge that I began to receive in my spirit about kairos moments has set me on a journey toward that God/Adam type relationship that I hunger for. And I believe that I am better equipped now to have that relationship than I have ever been in my life. And I also believe that the reason I am better equipped is that I have begun to watch for and prepare for kairos moments as I come to them. I now consciously look for those paths that move me closer to God. And at the same time I am more careful to avoid the other paths ... not paths that are necessarily sinful paths, but any path that takes me anywhere other than closer to God.

And that is what this chapter is really all about. It is a glimpse at other stories and other lives and how the small kairos' in their lives influenced how they handled the larger crossroads when they came to them. Some of those people made the good choices and moved ahead in the kingdom of God. Others made poor choices and started down a path that led them farther from God. But to me, the important part was not always what happened at those major crossroads, but what happened at the smaller ones all along the way ... *the things that brought them to and prepared them* for those truly defining moments in their lives.

CHAPTER 6

An Allegory

The Bible says that we are to give honor to whom honor is due. Right here, at the onset of this chapter, I would like to make some comments about my wife. If ever a person deserved commendation, it is my wife. I guess every woman and every man who has truly been blessed with a wonderful marriage believes that they have the very best of God's creations for a spouse, but they are wrong. I do. I can make one statement here that will put all other claims to rest. My wife still loves me after a four-year house remodel. I fancy myself to be an above average do-it-yourselfer. And with very little hesitation, and only a slight urging in my spirit, I moved my family to a disaster of a house over four years ago. My plans were to gut every room in the house and re-do them one room at a time, beginning with the closing in of the garage for a family room.

DECISIONS, DECISIONS, DECISIONS

Although we are almost finished now, and it has turned out even better than I had hoped, it was not always that way. My wife thought my beard had turned gray three years before it actually did because of the layer of construction dust that constantly covered me (and everything else)—and I am convinced that the reason it is gray now is because of the stress of living in a house while remodeling it. But the point is this; our marriage is better today than at any point in our lives. Those of you who have ever remodeled a house and lived in it at the same time know what that says. And that is a credit to her, not me. So let me use the words of Jackie Gleason and say, "Baby, you're the greatest."

The reason I want to get that said up front is so that you won't think this next statement is a criticism. In fact, Kimberlea will be the first to attest to the accuracy of this statement. My wife has no ability to visualize. Did I say *no* ability ... I meant *NO* ability to visualize; whereas I can just about see the end of a project before starting it. (What I *didn't* see was me getting burned out with construction work while maintaining my regular job, and the project taking four years instead of two). Our house is now fairly nice and sits toward the back of two acres outside of town. Where there had previously been only a weed patch, there are now two acres of solid grass. Where it had previously been empty acreage, it is now adorned with numerous lovely shade trees. After the house was almost done, I built a white two rail fence (which I had planned for before even closing on the house) to separate a yard area from the acreage area. She was not able to visualize what that fence would look like even after it was built. It was only after I put a coat of white primer on it that she said, "Oh, Honey, that fence is going to look really nice." So I had been enjoying my fence for four years before it was built, and she began to enjoy it after it was half painted—well, actually fully painted with one coat.

I have said all that to say this. I know there are many people who gain understanding more easily if they have a picture to look at. And a picture can be of benefit to any of us. It enables all of us to look at an object in the same way. Many of the ideas and statements in this book are somewhat abstract, and I feel it might help to draw a picture of what I am talking about. I won't draw an actual picture, but will try to draw a word picture.

Throughout this writing I have mentioned kairos moments and talked about them as crossroads, large and small, in our lives. I want to try to help you get a mental picture of that concept. It has helped me to look at it in this way. Now, every time I come to a kairos point in my life, an image of what I am about to describe pops up into my mind, actually making it easier for me to make a proper decision about which path to take. Jesus said that there are only two major roads upon which we can travel in this life. One of them he describes as a "broad" way with many travelers. This road leads to destruction. He describes the other road as a narrow one. Its entry ramp is small and it is hard to even find. In fact, compared to the other road, only a few people ever find this road. But for those who do find it, it will lead them to eternal life. As I describe these two roads, try to let the words create an image in your mind. If you can do that, this whole topic of kairos points will be much easier to grasp.

All of us have traveled on the broad way at some point, and may even be there now. The Bible says that we all start out our lives on that road. We don't have to look for the on-ramp; we are stationed there automatically by virtue of being the descendents of Adam. His sin, and that of Eve, put all of mankind on the road that leads to destruction. So picture a highway, wider than any you will find in Los Angeles. Along that highway are all the hospitals in the world where a human might be born. When they get to the age of travelling life's roads for themselves, the ramp from the hospital only feeds onto Broadway (the broad way). There is no ramp that goes straight to the narrow way. That road can only be traveled by decision after entering upon life's Broadway. For the sake of this book, we will not concern ourselves with what happens to those who die before being old enough to travel life's roads for themselves, because if you are reading this, that doesn't apply to you. Nor will we concern ourselves with the age at which it becomes possible for us to be responsible for our own actions on that road, because if you are reading this you are old enough to be accountable.

So here we are, all of us travelling down Broadway. Along this road, there are no sign ordinances like there are in many of our towns and cities. Anyone with anything to say or sell can place a sign along the road, advertising their wares, or services. Broadway is lined with these signs at off-ramps, or opportune spots ... kairos spots. Some are plain, maybe even hand drawn, and unobtrusive. Others light up the night because of the brightness of their neon. In addition to signs along the sides of Broadway, there are highway markers above the different lanes. They let you know ahead of time the lane you need to be in in order to get to the various locations. And because there are so many lanes marked with so many possible destinations, we are led to believe that these different lanes lead to *different* destinations. And because there are so many exit ramps that seem to be headed toward the places described on the signs, we are led to believe that these exit ramps will lead us to a *different* destination than the main highway will. But this is actually not true. Remember Jesus' quote from earlier in this chapter. There are only two roads and two destinations ... Broadway to Destruction, and Narrow Lane to Eternal Life. So even when a person takes an exit ramp from the main highway, she will end up at the same destination as she would have if she had not taken the exit ramp ... only two roads—only two destinations. Now these side roads will lead to different experiences along life's way, both on Broadway and Narrow Lane, but each only leads to one destination. They determine where we are *at any given moment* in this life, but as long as we are on that road, we are headed for one destination. Looking at it in this way means that we are not actually coming to crossroads as such, but are rather taking differing lanes on the highway, or are taking side roads that run parallel to the highway but which end up at the same place as the highway. This is actually a more accurate way of describing our kairos points than calling them crossroads. Our kairos moments actually come when we see an exit sign or a lane change sign and make a decision about which way to go.

Now, there is one other sort of exit that is available all along the way. It doesn't make any difference where you are on Broadway, there are off ramps that will take you over to Narrow Lane. And, depending on your theology (which we won't get into here), there may be off ramps from Narrow Lane which will take you back to Broadway. The reason I am skipping that discussion is not because I don't consider it important, but rather, because it is not the topic of this book and will serve no purpose here. This word picture will work for you no matter which way you believe.

Now it seems to me that the inclination might be to say, "Well, if off ramps to Narrow Lane are readily available all along the way, it is not terribly important for me to be in a hurry to get off Broadway and get over onto Narrow Lane." But let me finish my description and you will see why that is not the best choice.

Let's take a traveler from the time he is old enough to make his own travelling decisions and follow him for a ways—maybe not to the end of his journey, but for part of it. Just as would be the case with a teenager with his newly obtained driver's license, Traveler is filled with emotions which are new to him.

He has a sense of freedom and of possibilities. He is exhilarated by the power of being in control of his own life. True, he has (hopefully) some apprehensions as he starts out, but they are overshadowed by his eagerness to get on with his journey. As he eases from the on-ramp onto Broadway (his only choice because he is of Adam's race) he accelerates slowly in order to get the feel of life. He stays in the right hand lane because he is comfortable being near the shoulder.

Traveler has set out on his life journey. And on Broadway there are wonderful things to enjoy, and there are other travelers ... millions of them, both men and women ... and of all races and ages. In fact, as far as he can see, there are travelers. Some are so distant from him that he will likely never encounter them personally. Some are so distant that he never even sees them at all or knows that they exist. Some, like him, are still near the beginning of their on-ramp and others have traveled for some distance and are near the end of Broadway. Even though he knows others exist beyond his field of vision, Traveler can only see those in his immediate area. It is a truly wondrous place to him.

Here in this far right-hand lane, things seem only good. People are kind and honest. They are willing to help others when they see the need. Many of them even seem willing to go out of their way to do a timely good deed. They are generous and compassionate and care about their fellow travelers. In fact, there is so much apparent goodness here that there would hardly seem to be any reason to ever leave Broadway at all, or even to change lanes as far as that goes. And while Traveler occasionally sees someone exit at an obscure off-ramp to go over to Narrow Lane, he doesn't have much desire to go there himself. He can actually see over to that road, but it doesn't have a lot of traffic. Surely if it was a better place to be, it would be more heavily trafficked than it is. Besides, what could be better than this road? There are so many possibilities and options here. As Traveler looks across the way he sees that the Lane runs almost parallel to Broadway anyway. He figures they will both end up in the same place eventually. An exit to Narrow is coming up on his right, but he decides to pass by it and stay on Broadway. Traveler has just encountered his first major kairos and made a decision at it ... never realizing that it was an important decision at all.

By now Traveler has been on the road long enough that he is relaxed and less apprehensive. He feels in control of his journey and is comfortable that he can avoid a crash. He has seen some of the same people over and over again and has become friends with them. His journey is more pleasant because of them. But as his comfort level and confidence increase, he begins to pay more attention to the signs and the people in the other lanes. He notices that the people in the lanes farther to his left are travelling faster than he is. They seem to be enjoying more of what Broadway has to offer than he is. And some of the signs along the way and over their lanes are awfully enticing. He wonders about them but stays to the right ... another kairos—another decision. This one though was a good choice. It didn't take him over to Narrow Lane, but it was still one of the better choices he could make while on Broadway.

Not far down the road Traveler notices a girl about his age. He has seen her a couple of times before. She is only one lane over to the left from where he is and she smiles as she passes by him. Then, still in her lane, she slows down and allows him to catch up to her, only to speed back up and leave him behind again. He decides to try to catch up to her but the traffic in his lane moves pretty slowly. He gains a little ground on her but can never quite catch her because the other travelers in his lane are just too slow. He has never left the lane next to the shoulder before and it always seemed a comfort to him that he only had to worry about bumping into travelers on one side of him. But he sure would like to catch up to that girl, and maybe even get to know her. She does not slow down again and Traveler realizes that if he wants to catch her, he will have to speed up. He looks in his mirror and over his shoulder and eases left into her lane. He can go faster here and so he doesn't lose any more ground, but there are other travelers between him and her so he still can't catch her. He had never noticed it before, but the travelers in the next lane to his left are going quite a bit faster than the lane he just moved to. In fact, they are going quite a bit faster than he really wants to go. "Maybe I could just get over into that lane for long enough to catch up to her and then I will get back into this lane, either just in front of her or right behind her." He is a little scared to think about going as fast as the travelers in that next lane, but he waits for an open spot, speeds up and moves over yet one more lane to the left. There are now two lanes between him and that comfortable shoulder. But it is not as scary as he thought it might be and he knows that he won't be so scared if he decides to visit this lane again later. He speeds up to stay with the flow of the traffic in his lane. Sure enough, he catches up to her in no time, and not wanting to be a follower, he pulls back into her lane just in front of her. She flashes her lights at Traveler and they pull into a restaurant to get to know each other.

Traveler learns that the girl's name is Companion. Almost immediately they both realize that they have some special feelings for one another. And while Traveler has had very few significant experiences since his entry onto Broadway, Companion has been on her way a little longer. She has also spent a little time over in the faster lanes. But not only that, she had even taken a side road to visit a church ... more than once. There are lots of churches along Broadway but they all seemed to ramp right back up onto Broadway. Companion said that every time she had visited one, the only way out of the parking lot was back up onto Broadway. But she had heard that it was possible to get from the churches over onto Narrow Lane. In fact, that was what the churches were about—getting people to quit traveling Broadway and to move over to the Lane. Traveler had questions about her visits there. He wasn't sure why he had questions, but there was something inside him that made him curious.

For awhile the two of them were content to travel along Broadway near each other. Then they could stop and spend time together anytime they wanted to. They each gained new experiences as they went, some individually and others together. From time to time they would venture over into the faster lanes for excitement, but they always came back to stay near the two or three right-hand lanes. After a short time it became obvious that the two of them were very similar to one another, and for sure they were drawn to one another. Finally, Traveler asked Companion if they could travel together for the rest of their journey. It seemed only natural since they had so many similarities and likes and dislikes. *With no hesitation* whatsoever, Companion consented ... and a kairos passed unnoticed. The success or failure of the moment could only be known over the next years of time.

Traveling together this way had advantages. For one, loneliness was eliminated. Then too, they could pool their resources and enjoy more of the things that Broadway had to offer. There were concerts and amusement parks. There were ballgames and plays. There were cruises to be taken and gambling resorts. Most of the things they enjoyed doing were well to the right of the left-most lanes on Broadway. They had learned that the lanes to the far left were best avoided. Other people they talked to said that the people who traveled there were flying through life at breakneck speeds, seemingly in a hurry to get to the end of the road. And the lane signs above them advertised things that neither Traveler nor Companion was interested in ... things like recreational drugs and unnatural sexual involvement and organizations whose members seemed almost evil—who reportedly committed most of the crimes on Broadway. This couple though, was content to stay pretty much in the right-hand lanes where the people and experiences were more pleasant. In fact, they were downright enticing.

It wasn't long until Companion discovered she was pregnant. Both she and Traveler recognized this as an important point in their lives. As they talked about what this would mean to their lifestyle, they discovered that they had different opinions about what to do. Traveler, while wishing that this had occurred a little farther along the way, was at least a little excited about being a father. But not Companion. She had begun to cling to the fun they were having. A baby would rob her of her youthful years. By the time she had reared a child, the things that brought her pleasure now would have lost their attraction. She didn't want to bear the child. Traveler loved her so much and wanted her to be happy. So they decided, each for a different reason, to terminate the pregnancy ... kairos moments failed.

Whereas Traveler had been in favor of having the child, once the decision to terminate it was made, he never gave it much thought. They could always have another child later. But he was a little surprised to see how Companion changed. Whereas she was the one who had argued *not* to have a child at this time, she was the one that was bothered most by the decision. She seemed to have lost her joy for life. When Traveler shared the thoughts that had brought him consola-tion—that they could have another child anytime they wanted to—Companion could only say, "I know, but we can never have *that* child later." And for awhile she passionately did the things that had brought enjoyment to Traveler and herself ... the things that had helped her make the decision she had made in the first place. But they no longer attracted her the way they had, and Companion became despondent.

Even though the abortion itself did not bring a change to Traveler's demeanor or his enjoyment of life, the change in Companion did weigh on him. She had lost interest in the things that had formerly been a source of bonding for them. Oh, she wasn't totally depressed, but her joy was gone. She seemed to spend a lot more time "inside herself" than she had before. And when she was like that, things were not as natural between them. He missed her, the real her, the former her. And after awhile it was clear to both of them that they were drifting apart. Their souls seemed to no longer be united. Their emotional bond was damaged, and so was their physical relationship. They were still in those two or three right-most lanes where life had been so pleasant for them, but something was different, and not as pleasant.

Not long after that, Companion asked Traveler for something that surprised him. She asked him if they could go to church. They had gone before, but not recently ... not since the pregnancy. And when they had gone previously it was not out of a strong desire on the part of either of them, but rather, out of curiosity; they had just talked about it and decided to see what it was all about. But once they had visited, Traveler decided it wasn't worth giving up his Sundays for ... and the unusual curiosity he had previously felt seemed to diminish. Something was different this time though. He still had no interest in going, but the way Companion asked him made him know it was important to her. He was willing to try almost anything to get things back to the way they had previously been between them. They took the next church off-ramp they came to. This church was a little different than the one they had been to before. The people seemed glad, rather than just curious, to be there. And Companion learned that most of them were actually travelers on Narrow Lane. And what she had learned before was correct— there were ramps from the church over onto Narrow Lane, and there were ramps from both Broadway and Narrow Lane that led to the churches. The people who came to church from Broadway generally left that way, since they were already parked on that side anyway, and the same was true of those who entered from Narrow Lane. From time to time though someone would arrive on the Broadway side and leave on The Lane. And whereas previously Traveler had been the curious one, but decided he didn't want to give up his Sundays, now Companion had a renewed interest. After that one visit, she knew she would want to go back more and more. And she did—sometimes with Traveler and sometimes without. Her heart was happier, but the rift between the two seemed to be growing greater and greater.

It came to a point that Companion went to church every Sunday. Sometimes Traveler went too, but less and less. One morning when both of them were there, something seemed to take place in each of their hearts. At the end of every service there was both an urging and an opportunity for those traveling on Broadway to leave that road, and switch over to Narrow Lane. They said the reason that this was advisable was because of the final destinations of each of the two roads ... one to Destruction and one to Life. They had never made the switch before because it didn't really seem to either of them that their road was headed to Destruction. But lately Companion had become worried that they might be right. And, too, the people on Narrow did seem to always have that joy for life that she had had once. But that seemed long ago and she wanted it back. Anyway, on this particular morning, when they invited people to make the switch, both of them felt an unusual stirring in their heart ... a feeling that made them want to actually *make that switch*. Companion looked at her darling Traveler while everyone was bowed. She gave his hand a little tug, but he was rigid and didn't open his eyes. With a broken heart and tears streaming down her cheeks, she made a decision. She knew they would never make it as a pair if something didn't change. She knew she was not happy the way she was. She knew it might not work out, but she had to find out. As if severing a part of her own body she released her hand from Traveler's and started up the aisle to where she knew she would find the ramp to Narrow Lane. And as the service ended, at the point that she assumed she would enter The Lane, she was surprised to find that they ushered her back out the side of the church that she had come in ... the

Broadway side. She was about panicked and asked an usher why she was sent this way when her heart told her that she no longer belonged there.

The usher said, "Well, I suppose you can go out the other side if you want. But Traveler won't be on that side. If you still want to travel together, you will have to go to him until he is willing to come to you. Most married couples do it this way, at least for awhile."

"But doesn't that mean that I will still be traveling the wrong way," Companion asked?

"Well, you would think that, but God's ways are so much better than ours. You see, while you may still be traveling on Broadway in your body, your heart will be on Narrow Lane. And you will want to conduct yourself in the way that others on Narrow Lane conduct themselves. But God is more a God of the heart than he is of the body. As long as He knows your heart is with Him, He will allow your body to travel along with Traveler. After all, you did make a commitment to Traveler until death didn't you?"

Companion knew the usher was right. And *she had made that commitment* to Traveler, and she was glad, because she still loved him so much. In fact, it seemed that she loved him more at this very minute than she ever had before. But one thing was still bothering her. She told the usher, "Lately Traveler has been going places and doing things that I have no interest in. Things that the church says are not done on Narrow Lane. What if he wants me to go to those places and do those things?"

"Just ask God to give you wisdom each time one of those situations comes up," Usher answered back. "He may tell you to go to some of them, and He may not. Just ask with a pure heart. And if you don't join Traveler at some of the places he goes, don't hold that up in front of him. Don't criticize him for the things he does. Just continue to love him, and live in a Godly way in front of him. Ask God to change his heart the way He is changing yours. Who knows? There may come a day that Traveler will have a change of heart himself, and come over to The Lane."

Companion met Traveler outside the church and they set out on their way, Companion knowing that she would be returning to church every chance she got, and Traveler knowing he didn't ever want to come back. Neither of them said that to the other, but there was something different and they both knew it. Neither of them really understood it, but their hearts were not in tune the way they had been before. But there was one good thing about this whole deal; Traveler noticed that Companion finally seemed to be able to shake the depression that had been plaguing her lately. But the benefit of that was short lived as that barrier, or wall, or lack of unity, or whatever it was, began to take a toll on their already struggling union. It seemed to Traveler that all Companion wanted to do anymore was to go to church. While he, on the other hand, had begun to travel in the lanes to the left more and more frequently. He didn't intentionally plan it that way, but he was increasingly dissatisfied with the life he had at home. Companion was hardly a companion at all anymore.

DECISIONS, DECISIONS, DECISIONS

And in his going Traveler began to be tempted by other companionship that presented itself on Broadway. Oh, he didn't give in, it's just that now he entertained the thought rather than just casting it aside. Meanwhile, though not accompanying Traveler on many of his "recreational" excursions, Companion was a better wife than she had ever been. There might be places she would no longer go with her traveling companion, but she made the decision that in the home she would do all she could do to recognize what pleased him and to do those things. There may be a strange alienation between them, but if he left her, it wouldn't be because she drove him away. If she could find a way to get him to change over to Narrow Lane she was going to do it. And that included letting Traveler know she wished he would go to church with her, yet at the same time, not nagging him to go.

Companion began to learn things in the church ... things that made increasingly larger changes in her life and heart. One thing that she really began to appreciate was how wondrous it was that she—that anybody—came to travel on Narrow Lane. There were fun things to do but there wasn't much of the tinsel and glitter along it that there was on Broadway. There were attractions but not true enticements. In fact, most of the things to be truly appreciated about Narrow Lane didn't become evident until you had actually traveled on it. And even then the things that people came to appreciate were not the same sort of things that had made them enjoy Broadway. It wasn't a "doing" place; it was a "being" place. But her "being" was so much better here that she wanted more than anything to get Traveler to join her.

Another thing she learned was that many of the people on Narrow Lane had not come there through the church. Nor had many of them come there by means of the small, poorly marked on-ramps that led from Broadway over to the Lane. Many of them actually came there as a result of being in a wreck on Broadway. In the church she had met several who had told her stories of what it was like on the very fastest lanes on Broadway, the ones to the far left where she had never dared to travel. One of them had explained why it was so hard to get from there to Narrow Lane. He had said, "When you are traveling that far to the left on the highway it is a long way over to the exit ramps on the right that lead to the Lane. Even when a person begins to have a change of heart when she is way over there, there are lanes and lanes of traffic that she must cross over to get to the off-ramp. By the time they get part way over, they are often already past the exit. Many, many times a person will start trying to get over to the right from where they are and just give up because it is so hard to get through all the travelers in the right hand lanes of Broadway. That is where the mainstream of travelers stay. So while they may get uncomfortable with where they are and start moving to the right, they have several things to hinder them. First, the entice-ments of the fast lanes draw them back. Then they find that they are not happy going at the slower pace. They decide that if they are not comfortable in the slower lanes of Broadway, they surely wouldn't be happy if they got all the way off and went to Narrow Lane. So they just give up and stay where they are. It seems that just about the only way for those people to get off the fast lanes and have the opportunity to switch roads is to be in a wreck. What happens is that they are traveling in the drug lane, or the alcohol lane, or in compulsive gambling, or sexual deviancy or some of the other lanes and they crash. It can be a physical crash or an emotional one, or one of some other sort. It doesn't matter what type it is ... it is a life stopping, life changing wreck. Many, in fact most, of them die in the wreck. But for some, it is one last chance to get off of Broadway and onto the Lane. See, when they crash, physically or mentally or in whatever way, the emergency vehicles come. Traffic is stopped while they are being picked up out of the road and carried to the hospital. As it turns out, while they are recovering and trying to get their life straightened out, they discover that the recovery area is somewhat like the church. By that I mean that you can leave it and go back onto Broadway, or you can leave out of it on the other side and go onto Narrow Lane. Many people get to the Lane by making a decision while they are in the "wrecked life" recovery rooms. And for those who do go back out onto Broadway, if they aren't in a hurry to get back to the fast lanes, they will see the churches on the right, and they will stop in. Or they will see the off-ramps to the right before it is too late to exit and they will make their way over to Narrow Lane without ever spending much more time on Broadway. The only problem with that though is that many are killed in their wreck and never get a chance to leave the hospitals."

All of this stirred mixed emotions in Companion because she knew her Traveler was spending more and more time over in the left lanes. The talk gave her a bit of hope because it made her realize that it was at least possible to get from where he was to Narrow Lane. But it also brought an urgency because she realized that the possibility of him dying while on Broadway was great. She made a decision to pray more earnestly for Traveler ...

And that is where we will stop our story because the purpose never was to write a story but to draw a picture that you could store in your mind. Ever since I began to ponder this image, it jumps into my mind at every opportunity. I am making my life decisions from a different point of view. I know it won't be of benefit to everyone, but if it helps some, like my wife, it will have been worth the time and space.

I hope you will find a time to read back through this little story. It is filled with kairos points for both Traveler and Companion. Some of them are large and obvious; others are much smaller, but have an impact when a larger moment is reached. Some may not recognize anything about their life in this story, but I think most will at least be able to associate their life with some of the events. And the funny thing about this story is this ... I could have picked out any two of the millions of travelers that Traveler and Companion saw along Broadway and told their story instead. And if I had, it would have been totally different, because no two journeys are the same. And yet the story would also have been almost exactly the same because the outcome is the same for all of us. There are only two roads ... and only two destinations. Our reactions at kairos moments do two things. One, they determine which road we travel on; and, they determine the experiences, both good and bad, that we will encounter along our way. Although most of us have gone through our lives without ever even giving them any thought, kairos moments define our journey.

CHAPTER 7

The Next Step

I realize that my analogy is far from perfect. There can be no precise picture of how we actually travel through life. But it was a description that Jesus used, and I have only created details for it in order to help me get a mental picture of how I got to where I am. Hopefully that picture will also help me get to where I want to be. But there is a feature about life's journey that Traveler and Companion never got involved in; and perhaps most of us have never gotten involved in either ... at least not intentionally.

Throughout our story, and probably throughout our journey, we have usually just taken what came our way in life. That is not to say we have never been pro-active with regard to our future, but I am talking about the spirit world right now. In the natural we often create our own opportunities. I have a friend who knew since he was a youngster that he wanted to be an ophthalmologist when he grew up. Although I neither knew him or my mother-in-law until many years later, they knew each other. My mother-in-law was his English teacher in high school. After I married my wife, her mom sometimes talked about remembering hearing my friend say way back forty years earlier that he was going to be an ophthalmologist. And he is today. In fact, he is as dedicated to his profession as anyone I know. He still loves what he does and spends countless hours staying on the "cutting edge" of eye care technology. So I have to ask this question. Did he get to be where he is by taking life as it came to him, or did he get there by creating opportunities for himself?

If you remember back to the first chapter, we talked about three different types of kairos moments. There are those which are strictly in the natural realm, those which are strictly of a spiritual nature and those where the spirit world and the natural world interact. With my friend, there was nothing spiritual involved in becoming an ophthalmologist. But that doesn't mean that there were no kairos' in his life. And that is the key topic of this chapter. While our kairos decisions are what determine our destiny ... they are the decisions that have brought us to where we are ... and they are the defining moments of our lives; it is possible to *create some of our own moments* rather than just encounter life as it comes to us. My friend did this and achieved his childhood goal. *But we can do the same thing in the spirit and achieve a spiritual goal.*

There is a verse in the Psalms that I love. I

don't necessarily always live up to its lofty heights, but it is what I reach for. And although the verse is really describing the handiwork of God, and not the actions of man, I believe it can apply. In speaking of the sun being one of God's majestic creations, it says:

> **... In the heavens he has pitched a tent for the sun, which is like a bridegroom coming forth from his pavilion, like a champion rejoicing to run his course. (Ps. 19:4-5)**

In describing the sun's journey across the sky each day, he compares it to a "champion, rejoicing to run his race". Think about that and try to visualize it in your mind. If you arc a sports fan of any sort, you know what he is saying. And it doesn't matter what sport it is. Make sure though that you distinguish from the pseudo cockiness that we so often see displayed by athletes ... usually the ones who are not necessarily the true champions. They use their "game face" and their "smack talk" to try and intimidate their opponents. Forget them; that is not what makes a champion. I am talking about the true greats. They have a confidence that doesn't have to be created. You can see it on them, but it isn't something that they have to put on; it is something that rises up from within them. Yes, they might be beaten on any given day, but if they are, they know it will take the best effort of the best opponent to do it ... and they are not afraid of the challenge. They want the challenge. Something rises up within them and says, "Bring on anyone you want to. I am ready to run this race." The "best" don't have to display their confidence or their excitement for a challenger. It comes from within them and is part of how they walk and who they are. And it doesn't just apply to sports; it can be anything. In every activity, whether it is business, or sales, or acting, or driving a bulldozer, or directing traffic, or ... anything, there are those who excel in their area of endeavor. And they are not afraid to step in front of a crowd and do what they do. They rejoice to run their race, so to speak. It can be, and is, the same in the spirit world.

Do the people who attain this level of excellence get there just by making good and wise decisions at the crossroads of life? Well, making wise decisions certainly helps, but there is more to it. Making wise decisions will help keep us from straying off onto wrong paths. They will help us get to the end of our journey in the palm of God's hand. But they won't necessarily turn us into champions. That requires something more. That requires us to go back to what I said earlier about, "a more excellent way." If you remember, I used that term in describing how it was more desirable, and a better way, to learn to hear and follow God's voice than it was to have Him guide us by bit and bridle. But I also said in that chapter, that *in virtually every aspect of life*, I believed there was a more excellent way of doing things than what I am currently doing them. That doesn't just include hearing God, but it includes the handling of kairos moments in our life.

A good and proper way—a way that is almost certainly perfectly acceptable in God's eyes—is to call out for wisdom at each and every crossroad, or kairos, in our lives. When we get to them we stop and remember that we will encounter both Wisdom and Folly there, each of them calling out to us. We choose to follow Wisdom and head on up our straight and good path. God blesses us for the decision we made and we move on to our next kairos, better off, and better prepared as we go. How could God be displeased with that? He couldn't; and I believe that that will earn you a "well done" every time. But is there a "more excellent way"? Having done that, have we done all we can do to "be all that we can be"? Remember, we talked about that being our goal earlier. I stated then that I am not writing this to nominal Christians, but to those who want to *be* all, and to *do* all that they possibly can in, and for, the kingdom of God, for as long as God will allow them to. And for those people, I want to say that there is indeed more that we can do. The "more" thing that we can do is this. Instead of waiting for kairos moments to come our way and then choosing well at them, *we can begin to actually create kairos moments in our lives that will take us places that we never would have gone if we had simply waited for a kairos to come to us.*

Let's look at an Old Testament example of someone who did just that. We find the story in the 19th chapter of 1 Kings.

So Elijah went from there and found

Elisha son of Shaphat. He was
plowing with twelve yoke of oxen,
and he himself was driving the
twelfth pair. Elijah went up to him
and threw his cloak around him.
Elisha then left his oxen and ran after
Elijah. "Let me kiss my father and
mother good-by," he said, "and then
I will come with you."
"Go back," Elijah replied. "What
have I done to you?"
So Elisha left him and went back. He
took his yoke of oxen and slaughtered them. He burned the plowing
equipment to cook the meat and gave
it to the people, and they ate. Then
he set out to follow Elijah and
became his attendant.

What we have here is the calling of Elisha as
prophet to replace Elijah. We don't know much about
Elisha prior to this but we can assume that he was a
God fearing man. We can assume that his heart was
inclined toward hearing and obeying the voice of God.
That gives me ground for hope, because I have those
qualities. I have a love and a reverential fear for God.
I strive to hear and obey His voice. I believe you have
those characteristics. And if you do, then you are on a
path that will lead you to an encounter with God.

Think with me for just a minute about what
happened here, and then we will read more. Elijah,

arguably the greatest prophet to have lived, is approaching the end of his earthly ministry. God has instructed him to anoint Elisha to take his place. Elijah does this symbolically by draping his cloak over Elisha. This was a symbol that the anointing mantle that had rested on Elijah would, at the proper time, come to rest on Elisha. Why did God select Elisha? We don't know but it can be assumed that God saw something in his spirit that was useable. But whatever it was, it was a quality that God appreciated. Now, when this event was over, Elisha did not immediately assume the position of Prophet of Israel. In fact, he asked permission to go home and say good-bye to his parents. In his culture, that could take from days to weeks. Elijah told him to go ahead and go, but that he should keep in mind what he (Elijah) had done to him. It was a situation similar to what happened with David when Samuel anointed him king. It actually took several more years before David assumed the throne. But from that point on, David, as well as others, knew that David would one day be king. So from that point on, Elisha knew he had a destiny in the kingdom of God. Does that sound in any way familiar? Have you felt that in your own life? I think you have. I feel it in my own life as well. Will it be some big obvious ministry? Who knows! But it doesn't matter. What matters is that we discover and fulfill that spiritual destiny, whatever it may be. Well, Elisha went home and began to make preparations for his calling. And let me say some things here that took place in Elisha's heart and mind that would be of benefit to us as well. When Elijah anointed Elisha as his replacement, God created a set kairos in Elisha's life. He *would* be the next prophet of Israel. Did God place any requirements on Elisha in order for that to come true? No. It would have been possible for Elisha to remain in his home area and await the fulfillment of that promise. But is that what Elisha did? No! What did he do? He made up his mind that if being the Prophet of Israel was his destiny, then he wanted to "be all that he could be" in that position. He went home and burned all the bridges (actually farming implements) that tied him to his old way of life. He even slaughtered his oxen and gave a feast for his neighbors. Then he went and became Elijah's assistant, or servant. Well, what is one of the principles in God's kingdom? If we want to become great in the kingdom, we must be servants. Elisha immediately took this first of several steps to ensure the quality of his Godly calling. He didn't wait for his kairos to come to him; *he set out to create even better kairos opportunities than what were in store for him anyway.*

Now, we really don't hear anything else about Elisha until the 2nd Book of Kings. There we find that the time has finally come for God to take Elijah up to heaven and for Elisha to assume his position as prophet. He had made the decision earlier to begin preparing himself for that position. Elijah knew it, and either because Elijah told him or else God told him, Elisha knew it too, as did the other prophets in the area. A major kairos was just around the corner. What Elisha didn't know was that there were several smaller kairos' coming before the big one. All of these smaller kairos' had the potential for preventing Elisha from ever getting to the big kairos for which he had been preparing. Let's look at the story. It takes up a large part of 2 Kings 2.

When the LORD was about to take Elijah up to heaven in a whirlwind, Elijah and Elisha were on their way from Gilgal. Elijah said to Elisha, "Stay here; the LORD has sent me to Bethel."
But Elisha said, "As surely as the LORD lives and as you live, I will not leave you." So they went down to Bethel.
The company of the prophets at Bethel came out to Elisha and asked, "Do you know that the LORD is going to take your master from you today?"
"Yes, I know," Elisha replied, "but do not speak of it."
Then Elijah said to him, "Stay here, Elisha; the LORD has sent me to Jericho." And he replied, "As surely as the LORD lives and as you live, I will not leave you." So they went to Jericho.
The company of the prophets at Jericho went up to Elisha and asked him, "Do you know that the LORD is going to take your master from you today?"
"Yes, I know," he replied, "but do not speak of it."
Then Elijah said to him, "Stay here; the

LORD has sent me to the Jordan."
And he replied, "As surely as the LORD
lives and as you live, I will not leave you."
So the two of them walked on.
Fifty men of the company of the prophets
went and stood at a distance, facing the
place where Elijah and Elisha had
stopped at the Jordan. Elijah took his
cloak, rolled it up and struck the water
with it. The water divided to the right
and to the left, and the two of them
crossed over on dry ground.
When they had crossed, Elijah said to
Elisha, "Tell me, what can I do for you
before I am taken from you?"
"Let me inherit a double portion of your
spirit," Elisha replied.
"You have asked a difficult thing," Elijah
said, "yet if you see me when I am taken
from you, it will be yours—otherwise not."
As they were walking along and talking
together, suddenly a chariot of fire and
horses of fire appeared and separated the
two of them, and Elijah went up to
heaven in a whirlwind. Elisha saw this
and cried out, "My father! My father! The
chariots and horsemen of Israel!" And
Elisha saw him no more. Then he took
hold of his own clothes and tore them
apart.
He picked up the cloak that had fallen

from Elijah and went back and stood
on the bank of the Jordan. Then he
took the cloak that had fallen from him
and struck the water with it. "Where
now is the LORD, the God of Elijah?"
he asked. When he struck the water, it
divided to the right and to the left, and
he crossed over.
The company of the prophets from
Jericho, who were watching, said, "The
spirit of Elijah is resting on Elisha."
And they went to meet him and bowed
to the ground before him.

Do you see the full story of what happened
here? Elijah and Elisha are travelling along together on
foot. They both know that the time has come for Elijah
to depart. Elijah turns to Elisha and says something to
the effect of, "Elisha, your time is coming. But I have
a couple of loose ends to tie up before I go. God has
told me to go to Bethel. There is no reason for you to
go though, so you can just stay here." But Elisha knew
in his heart that he had been preparing himself for
something more than just a casual farewell from his
mentor. And although the Bible doesn't say so, the
ponderer inside me believes that Elisha already had
something in his heart regarding how he wanted things
to end up. He was at a significant kairos in his life ... a
kairos that would have a significant impact on whether
or not he ever came to the really big kairos that he
hoped for. He told Elijah "no way." If Elijah was going

somewhere at God's command, Elisha was going too. So they headed off to Bethel together.

Now there was a school for the prophets at Bethel. The prophets there asked Elisha if he knew what was about to happen. He said he did but he didn't want to talk about it. In awhile Elijah told Elisha, "Well, now God has told me to go on to Jericho. But here are the young prophets. You will be the head of them. You might as well just stay here and go ahead and assume your position." It was another significant kairos that would impact his future, and it would determine if he ever got to the really big kairos that he hoped for. He had something in his spirit and again he said "no way." If God was sending Elijah to Jericho, Elisha was going too. So the two of them went on together.

Now the same thing happened at Jericho as happened at Bethel. The school of prophets asked Elisha if he knew that his master was going to be taken away from him that day. Elisha said yes, but he didn't want to talk about it. Whatever it was in his spirit was between him and God. Sometimes when we believe that we have a promise from God in our hearts it is best to just be quiet about it and see what happens. About that time Elijah told Elisha that God had told him to go to the Jordan River. And again he told Elisha, "Look Elisha, I appreciate your loyalty. But here is this group of prophets. You will be the head of them. You might as well just go ahead and stay here and be the Prophet of Israel. I am about to be taken away anyway." It created yet another opportunity for Elisha to settle for the good blessings of God instead of holding out for the "best" that he could receive from God. He knew he had been preparing for something and he was going to see it through to the end. The worst that could happen if he was wrong about the hopes he had inside him was that he would take Elijah's place as prophet with God's blessing. He was willing to go that extra mile in hopes of receiving that something bigger that he felt stirring in his heart. "No, if you are going to the Jordan, I am going to the Jordan." And the two of them went on together.

When they got there Elijah knew that he was supposed to go to the other side so he rolled up his cloak and struck the Jordan with it. The waters parted and the two of them crossed over on dry ground. Elijah's time had come and Elisha was still with him. He turned and talked to Elisha. "Elisha, you have been a faithful servant and companion to me. It is time for me to go though. What can I do for you before I go?" Elisha had made the right decision at three consecutive kairos points. All of them were good points. He was about to receive the prophetic anointing of God no matter what he decided at any of those three points. But he believed in his heart that he had been preparing for something better. He had made decisions all along the way that indicated that he was willing to forego the good blessings of God in the hopes of receiving the best blessings of God. *Elisha wasn't just making good decisions at the kairos' of his life, he was creating other and better kairos'.*

I recognize that the situation with Elisha is a little different than it is with us, but the principle remains. It is good that we consult with God at our kairos moments. It will be wonderful if, when we get to the crossroads of life, both large and small, we begin to listen for the voices of Wisdom and Folly, so that we can distinguish between the two and make good choices. It will be great if we begin to choose paths that will lead us to yet more important kairos points. But there is still that "more excellent way." We, like Elisha, can begin to create kairos' that work to our own advantage. As to how to do that, a person would need to get before God and ask the Holy Spirit to show them things that will work in their own individual lives. But there are some spiritual principles that have been established that work in the life of anyone who will apply them.

What happens when you go to bed at night? What is your routine? It will vary because of different lifestyles. And since I have brought that up, I may as well go on and say that if, when it gets to be bedtime, you are in a relationship that is out of line with the Word of God, you are at a kairos. There will be no need to go any farther with your pursuit of God until those relationships are corrected. Is that an easy thing to do? No. But is it necessary? It is if you want to reach the place in God that I have been describing for all of these pages. But I did not bring up the subject of bedtime in order to be able to ask that question. The reason I brought it up was so that you would see how you create kairos moments everyday without thinking about it ... and that by thinking about it, you can create better ones.

So, back to our bedtime example. One of the things most of us do at bedtime is *set* the alarm clock.

When you set that clock you are making a decision that will effect more than just your ability to get to work or school on time. When you set that clock you are establishing some of the boundaries of your relationship with God. This is what I mean. Once a clock has been set, it usually remains that way for the entire workweek and probably for many workweeks to come. See if what I say here resembles the process you used when you set it for the first time.

"Okay now, I need to be at work at nine. And because I am a compulsive early arriver (or not) I want to leave in time to be there five minutes early (or late). It is an eighteen-minute drive in good traffic ... twenty-four in moderate (we won't allow for bad). Let's allow twenty. Now I can shower and get ready in twenty-two minutes if I have a breakfast drink on the way. So I need to get up at 8:15." Now I know all that is made up, but isn't that about how it usually works? We count backwards in minutes until we find the latest time that we can get up and still be where we need to be on time, or at least almost on time?

When we make the decision based on those criterion we have set ourselves on a certain path. And the path we chose was one that did not start out with God being a part of the beginning of the day. *Would we not have created* and entered upon at least a slightly different path if we had done all of those calculations and then added fifteen more minutes to it in order to spend a little devotional time with God at the beginning of the day? Or what if we added thirty minutes or two hours. Would our lives not then be on slightly different paths than they are when we get up just in time to make it to work? If you remember, the Bible says that often Jesus arose a great while before day to pray. What He was doing when He did that was to create kairos moments for His life. And if we do that we will create Godly kairos' for our lives as well. I know that time is our most valuable commodity in these hectic days. So it comes down to this. How badly do we want it? How serious are we about finding a deeper place in God than we have ever found before? We can settle for the good, or we can be like Elisha and hold out for more. But the point is that every night at bedtime we have an opportunity to create a kairos in our lives. In fact, when we set that alarm we are actually facing a kairos of sorts. It is not a kairos that we pass or fail, but it is one that determines what path we will walk on the next day. This isn't heaven or hell type of stuff. It isn't a matter of being saved or not. It is what I said at the outset—the deeper stuff ... the going on to maturity stuff ... and maybe even deeper than that stuff. It is the "be all you can be" stuff.

Well, actually it is not quite the "be all you can be" stuff, because there is even more. Do you remember that story in the Gospels where some of the disciples had tried to cast a demon out of a man, but couldn't? Jesus told them that some things could only take place by prayer *and* fasting. This is very similar to the alarm clock situation. Sometimes we make decisions by not making decisions. When we don't make the decision to set the alarm clock earlier, in order to have time to spend with God in the mornings, we are actually making the decision *not* to spend dedicated time with God in the mornings. How often do we make the decision to fast? Well, *every meal that we sit down to eat is a decision not to fast that meal.* Did we consciously decide not to fast? No. It is a decision by default. We didn't make the decision *to* fast, so by default we made a decision *not* to fast. I know this is hard stuff. But ask the Special Ops soldiers in our military if it was easy to get there. Ask any athletic champion if it was easy to get there. Ask any of the spiritual leaders in the church today if it was easy to get there. Or I will save you the labor of asking. It wasn't easy. It is never easy. Most of us will never know the effort and the struggle and the disappointments and the failures that went into becoming a champion. But how badly do we want it? I am not writing this to try to encourage you to pursue any of these paths. I only want to make sure that anyone who wants to walk on a higher path with God knows that there are in fact higher paths to walk on. I only want to make sure that anyone who is looking for a more excellent way, can know that there is one ... and that it can be attained. And we all need to know that when we get to that better way—there is yet a better and higher path that we can walk on. Oh, we may not be able to see it or even to imagine it from where we are now, but when we get to that next and better path, we will see yet a next and better path. And some of these paths are not to be found in the course of our everyday lives, but rather, the kairos' that lead to them *have to be created.* How badly do we want to find, or rather create, those paths? The answer to that question might be found by simply looking at your alarm clock ... or your fasting habits ... or any of a number of things that the Holy Spirit might show you. There are kairos' to be *encountered*— may we choose well when we arrive at them. But there are also kairos' to be *created*—may we choose to create them.

CHAPTER 8

The War

So, what do we have so far? As we live this life we encounter decisive moments which define our destiny. At those points we either follow Wisdom or Folly, both of whom stand at those crossroads trying to draw us toward them. If we are really aggressive in the kingdom of God we can actually begin to create our own kairos moments rather than to just encounter them as they come our way. In so doing we can begin to make gains in the kingdom of God by choice rather than by chance. Pretty simple, huh? Not really.

In Chapter 3 we introduced the discussion concerning the means by which Satan will attempt to divert anyone traveling along The Way. Simply by making Broadway appear more appealing than it is, and by making Narrow Lane appear more radical and unnecessary than it is, he is able to keep the majority of people on Broadway. But we have survived that. We have wanted more of God and we have taken steps to draw closer to Him. What can we expect? Well, in that 3rd chapter I referred to this struggle that we have with Satan as he tries to get us to travel the wrong paths as the "first battlefield" that he uses ... but I didn't refer to it as the only battlefield.

Let's talk for a few minutes about Satan—about what his nature is ... what his plans are ... and what his motives are. We have already mentioned that he is a brilliant, capable and extremely powerful enemy. "But," you might say, (and with good reason), "Jesus has defeated him and given me power over all the power of the enemy." And that statement is also true ... and I thank God it is true. But that has not made Satan less wise, or less powerful. It has only made it possible for us to be more wise and more powerful. For most of us, though, simply having "power over all the power of the enemy," while comforting to think about, is rarely worked out where it counts—in our day to day lives. If it were, there would not be virtually the same divorce rate in the body of Christ as there is in the general population. Far too often the power we have at our disposal is not being brought to bear in our actual lives. Could the reason that we don't reach the place in God that we want to reach be that we have failed to recognize the devices used by the one who would stop us from growing in God?

How do we fix that? What do we need to watch for? How do we avoid the destruction Satan has planned for us? The first thing we need to realize is that

Satan is not our enemy so much because of whom we are, but rather because he is an enemy with God. Apart from the fact that we have interest in God, Satan has no interest in us. It is not a very Christian attitude to take, but have you ever found yourself having feelings of dislike for someone simply because they were friends of another person that you didn't like, or were at odds with? That is how Satan is with God. God removed him from the position of High Guardian Cherub, and cast him out of the Kingdom of God. Satan seethes because of that. Ever since then, Satan has gone about seeking to steal, or kill, or destroy any work of God that he can. If he can steal a soul, he will do so because that is a slap in the face of God. His goal for the remainder of his free life is to destroy the work of God anywhere he finds it. When we, as human beings with souls on the line, begin to show an interest in the things of God, Satan resists us through a variety of means. The harder that we work to grow in the Grace of God, the more violently he behaves in his attempts to prevent that growth. He will not give up, and unless we give in, this conflict actually becomes a war. Let me show you. 1 Peter 5:8 says:

> **Be self-controlled and alert. Your enemy the devil prowls around like a roaring lion looking for someone to devour.**

That describes an act of war. When you openly declare that you are seeking to destroy a person or geographical location, you are declaring war on them.

DECISIONS, DECISIONS, DECISIONS

That is what Satan has done in regard to those who would pursue God or His Christ. As for our part, we are declared to be in a warfare to stop Satan's attacks. In 2 Cor. 10:3 we read:

> **For though we walk in the flesh, we do not war after the flesh: (For the weapons of our warfare are not carnal, but mighty through God to the Pulling down of strongholds;) Casting down imaginations, and every high thing that exalteth itself against the knowledge of God ... (KJV)**

We are in a warfare. It is generally spiritual in nature, and our only weapons are certainly spiritual. Sometimes the effects of Satan's raging will spill over into the physical world, but they can only be prevented, and he can only be resisted, by doing warfare in the spirit world. That principle applies whether we are talking about preventing his doing damage to us ... or if we are talking about us taking the offensive, and doing damage to him and his kingdom. You may not have ever reached the place where you were ready to pick fights with Satan. Most Christians, to our discredit, spend our lives just hoping that we can keep him from doing us in. The point where we are in this book now though is far beyond that. We are no longer in the defensive posture, fighting for our spiritual lives, but we are out to possess the ground that God has given us, and to gain new ground. There is a somewhat misunderstood verse in the Bible which partially explains this process. The verse can be, and is, explained in two totally different ways by different translators. In the KJV the verse says this:

> And from the days of John the
> Baptist until now the kingdom of
> heaven suffereth violence, and the
> violent take it by force. (Mat. 11:12)

While the NIV states it this way:

> From the days of John the Baptist until
> now, the kingdom of heaven has been
> forcefully advancing, and forceful men
> lay hold of it.

The two possible interpretations for this verse are:

1. There is warfare going on in the heavens and the Kingdom of Heaven is undergoing violent attacks. Those who would gain the kingdom must be forceful.

2. The kingdom of God has been advancing, but it is because men are willing to be forceful in their attempts to further the kingdom.

For the sake of this topic, it does not matter which interpretation is more accurate because either one will show us why making gains in the kingdom of God is not easy. Either interpretation shows that there is spiritual warfare going on in regard to the kingdom of God. And the scriptures are full of examples of that warfare. In fact, the scriptures not only give examples of the warfare, but they discuss the type of warfare that we face. In Ephesians 6:11-12 we find a verse that is similar to what we read in 2 Cor. It says:

> **Put on the full armor of God so that you can take your stand against the devil's schemes. For our struggle is not against flesh and blood, but against the rulers, against the author-ities, against the powers of this dark world and against the spiritual forces of evil in the heavenly realms.**

And look who has showed back up ... Wise Serpent ... the devil. What is he doing? He is scheming. He knows that he is in a warfare against the saints of God, and he is scheming. We can see another picture of it in 2 Cor. 2:10-11 where the Apostle Paul, in talking about forgiving someone in the church, had this to say.

> **... I have forgiven in the sight of Christ for your sake, in order that Satan might not outwit us. For we are not unaware of his schemes.**

Why is he scheming? If he is going to "devour" us, why doesn't he just do it and get it over with? Let's take a minute to re-visit some Biblical truths. 1 John 4:4 states, " ... greater is he that is in us than he that is in the world." (KJV) Greater in what way? Greater in every way. Greater in power. Greater in skill. Greater in wisdom. Greater in kingdom. Greater in every way. The one who lives in us is greater. Now if the greater one lives within us then we can not be defeated forcefully by the lesser one. So Satan can not use brute strength or force to defeat us. And yet, our defeat is his goal. Do you know of a Christian whom he has ever devoured ... either physically or spiritually? I do. Well, if he didn't do it by force or power, how did he do it? He did it by subtlety. He does it by creating opportunities for failure and by camouflaging those opportunities to look innocent or even desirable. And then, when we choose poorly at those crossroads, he has the upper hand. He also devours some unnecessarily by making his force seem greater than it is. He may hinder someone's prayer until they say, "Well, this disaster must be God's will." And when they reach that point, they quit standing firm in their faith, and they lose their battle. Did they lose because the One inside them was weaker than the one attacking them? No! The greater One lives inside them! The weaker one is on the outside attacking and seeing if he can find someone to devour. Can he devour anyone he wants to? No. He is going about as a lion *looking for someone that he can devour.* How does he know when he has found them? He exploits them and looks for weaknesses. He tempts them and examines their response. He tries them and determines whether they know their rights as believers or not. If he finds one who does not know the power that indwells them, he can bluff them into failure. If he finds one who is not aware of his scheming ways, he will defeat them through subtlety. He is the Wise Serpent and he is skillful in his methods of destruction.

You see, God allows Satan to see to it that there is not a man or woman who passes through the realm of humanity who is not tempted to violate the ways and will of God. He does it for a purpose. That is how He sees what we are made of, and probably just as importantly, that is how *He shows us* what we are made of. Jesus was no exception. Heb. 4:15 says that He was "... tempted in every way, just as we are—yet was without sin." Was He tempted for real, or was He just tempted with token temptations so that He could satisfy the demands required for being "tempted ... yet sinless"? They were the real thing. And they were presented by the one who would rather have caused *Him* to stumble than all of the rest of us put together. What kind of temptations? Every kind. With us, Satan is selective. For instance, there are those who never, for any reason, would be inclined to steal something. So, will that be the area that Satan is likely to use to cause them to stumble? Not likely. But do they have a weakness for pornography? Do they have a difficult time turning away from a movie or a website that plants seeds of lust in their hearts or minds? If they do, then Satan will attack along those lines. Are they impervious to temptations of lust? Well, what is their level of willingness to forgive when wronged unjustly? It is different for all of us. The temptations that disrupt the lives of others may not have any appeal to us at all. And they may not be tempted in the least by what draws us away. But we all have something. We are all plagued in some area of our lives. You know what yours are. No one else may even have a clue about them ... but you know. And I have them ... and I know. The apostle Paul had them, and he knew. And Wise Serpent knows what those weaknesses are—and he schemes and devises ways to exploit them.

Well, as I said, it was the same for Jesus, except that in order for His act of redemption to be legal in the eyes of God, He had to face them all—yours, mine and everyone else's. We have the story of how most of it came about. It is written in the book of Luke. The NIV catches very precisely what was given in the Greek.

Jesus, full of the Holy Spirit, returned from the Jordan and was led by the Spirit in the desert, where for forty days he was tempted by the devil. He ate nothing during those days, and at the end of them he was hungry.
The devil said to him, "If you are the Son of God, tell this stone to become bread."
Jesus answered, "It is written: 'Man does not live on bread alone.'"
The devil led him up to a high place and

showed him in an instant all the kingdoms of the world. And he said to him, "I will give you all their authority and splendor, for it has been given to me, and I can give it to anyone I want to. So if you worship me, it will all be yours."
Jesus answered, "It is written: 'Worship the Lord your God and serve him only.'"
The devil led him to Jerusalem and had him stand on the highest point of the temple. "If you are the Son of God," he said, "throw yourself down from here. For it is written: "'He will command his angels concerning you to guard you carefully; they will lift you up in their hands, so that you will not strike your foot against a stone.'"
Jesus answered, "It says: 'Do not put the Lord your God to the test.'"
When the devil had finished all this tempting, he left him until an opportune time. (Lk. 4:1-13)

Did you notice that last sentence? It said that the devil left Him until an *opportune time*. What do you suppose the Greek word for opportune time was that he used here? That's right! It is that word *kairos.* It means that Satan was giving up on Jesus for the moment, but he would try again later ... when a better opportunity presented itself. He would explore Jesus for any weak areas, and when an opportune moment came along, he would bring a new and more challenging temptation. Why would another time be more opportune than this particular moment? Because Jesus had just finished fasting for forty days. He was full of the Holy Spirit. It was a mountain top in His life. He had been able to withstand the temptation of being offered all the kingdoms of the world. Satan would watch for a weaker moment in Jesus' life. Do you see how this has now gone far beyond the point of just trying to misdirect us at a crossroad. It is overt scheming. If Jesus, or if we, are diverted at the cross-roads, Satan's job is done, and he has won. But if we persist, he becomes more vigorous in his attempts. He schemes and looks for opportunities.

So what would be that golden opportunity that Satan would be watching for in Jesus' life? We are not told. But we do know that more temptations came because there are some temptations that can't come to us alone in the desert. How about the group of women who were always a part of Jesus' following. We are told that Jesus loved Mary and Martha. Did Satan use them as a source of temptation? We know that Mary Magdalene was passionate about Jesus; was it her? We can't say for sure, but he used somebody, some woman. Else, He wasn't tempted in every way that we are. But the "fasting, mountaintop" time would not have been the opportune time for those. That would more likely come when He was lonely ... when He was tired and misunderstood. It would have come at a time when a woman, with her built in ability to perceive His moods, saw that He was pondering His role on this Earth. And the weight of that was heavy, and He was bearing it alone. And in a nurturing way, not brashly, but caringly, she would come and caress and comfort Him. That is a temptation that He would have had to face ... and Satan would have brought it at the opportune moment.

Do you think Satan left Jesus and just hoped that a good opportunity would present itself? No! He set about to create opportunities, subtle opportunities, for Jesus to fail. Because while in one sense Jesus *was* the greater one, while He was here on Earth He was like us. If it were not possible for Jesus to fail, the whole thing is rigged and His triumph a farce. But His temptations and trials were real, and He didn't fail. How did He do it? How did He succeed? He did it the same way we must ... He had the greater one living inside Him in the person of the Holy Spirit. That is how the Father communicated with Him while He was here. God rarely spoke to Him in person, but He was full of the Holy Spirit and heard from God in that way. It will need to be the same with us. We have to culti-vate that relationship with the Holy Spirit to where we instantly recognize it when He speaks to us. It is Satan's job to deceive us and to devour us. It is the Holy Spirit's job to guide us into all truth. And the Truth will set us free. Free from what? Free from all the scheming ways of the enemy.

I suspect that by now you are asking how this relates to the topic of this book. It is in this way. If we are in a warfare—and we are—then there can only be two possible outcomes to our battles. We can win or we can lose. Who determines which of those two it will be? We do. If it is impossible for Satan to defeat us by his strength, then it is only possible for him to defeat us by his devices. The number and the characteristics of those devices will be in proportion to the effort you put into your efforts to make gains in the kingdom of God. What I mean by that is this. Satan is not God and he is not like God. God is omniscient and omnipresent and omnipotent ... all-knowing, all-present and all-powerful. Satan is limited in all three of those areas. He is wise, but not all knowing. He is limited in his presence to the number of demons that he has in his control as eyes and ears. He is powerful, but less powerful than the one who lives inside us. So he has limited resources. But remember that he is wise. So he will not waste his resources. He will only deploy that amount of effort and power that he thinks he has to in order to accomplish his goals. But on the other hand, if he thinks he has a chance to win a battle, he will use all resources he has at his disposal to hinder a person from making gains in the kingdom of God.

Listen to me. God uses kairos moments to move us toward eternity. He considers them important. Jesus walked this life aware of kairos moments, and considered them important. Satan understands kairos moments, and conducts his business in line with them. He knows they are important. Does that not make it paramount that we begin to take a new look at these crossroads of time and space in our lives? It does. We will not realize our full spiritual potential until we begin to realize the mechanisms by which God deals with man and the mechanisms by which the enemy of our souls tries to destroy us. They both know the kairos moments in our lives and they are both in attendance at those points, hoping that when we get to the crossroad, we will choose their path.

If we are trying to make gains in the kingdom of God, we are in a warfare. We will not win that war unless a few things become a reality to us. First, we have to recognize that this war must be fought. We must be strong in spirit ourselves, and even more importantly we must be strong in the Spirit of God. Can we become strong in God's Spirit through a casual love for God, or through a casual distaste for the ways of Satan? No. This battle is not for the faint of heart ... and far too few will undertake it. It is fought at the crossroads of life—at the ones that Satan sends our way, and if we want it badly enough, at the ones we create for ourselves with the help of the Holy Spirit. Are you a warrior? I hope so. Although the cost may be high, it cannot remotely compare with the rewards.

CHAPTER 9

The Rewards

And what are those rewards? What is the gain that is so great that it would make our struggles with Satan worthwhile? The answers to those questions are not discoverable by me in your behalf. I know what the answers are for a few people, mostly Biblical characters. I know what the answers are in my own life. I know what the answers might be for a group of believers in a church who set themselves to pursue a closer relationship with God. But I don't know what they are for you. Let me explain and give some examples.

First, and I suppose foremost, is the reward of heaven. And that is attainable by any who are willing to make the correct and proper choice at a kairos that offers them the opportunity to follow God and walk along His pathway. And while the thrust of this book is

DECISIONS, DECISIONS, DECISIONS

directed toward those who have made a decision to go far beyond that initial good and proper choice, I do not want to slight that choice because of its dire consequences. We talked about the two paths and the fact that no matter how much we meandered while on them, each of them only had one destination. Two paths ... two destinations. But because those destinations are generally known, we did not state them as such. Lest there be a single soul who is unaware, let me state them here to show the most immediate benefit of choosing God's path. The Bible says in Mathew 7:13-14 that:

> ... wide is the gate and broad is the road
> that leads to destruction, and many
> enter through it. But small is the gate
> and narrow the road that leads to life,
> and only a few find it.

Broadway leads to destruction. Hell. Damnation. Eternal torment. Eternal separation from God. Eternal separation from all the loved ones who chose Narrow Lane. And the reward for choosing wisely at any kairos that presents itself along those lines is life. Eternal life. Access to the very tree of life. Eternity in the Presence of the Almighty God who rules and reigns the Universe in righteousness. Joy unspeakable and glory that can not be described. So if you never make another step toward God than just those that are necessary to stay on the narrow way ... at the very least make those good choices.

Beyond that the rewards are too individualized

to say what they might be except in the case of saints who have gone on before us and left us their stories. And their stories are numerous. The Old Testament character which most readily comes to my mind when I think of people who demonstrated a desire to serve God at any cost is King David. Did David make mistakes? Yes. Did that disqualify him for the reward? No. It could have, but he didn't allow it to. What riches there are ... what emotions there are ... what yearnings there are in the writings of David. Let me quote a few of them and together we will see if we can identify what prize David was shooting for as he pursued God. Yes, that is right, it was for a prize. And it is okay to pursue God for the prize ... just don't be surprised if the prize is different than what the world would normally call a prize. Look what Paul the Apostle said in his letter to the Philippians:

> **... I press on to take hold of that for which Christ Jesus took hold of me. Brothers, I do not consider myself yet to have taken hold of it. But one thing I do: Forgetting what is behind and straining toward what is ahead, I press on toward the goal to win the prize for which God has called me heavenward in Christ Jesus. (3:12-14)**

And what was that prize that Paul labored and suffered for? I am not sure, and the Word does not say specifically. If I were to venture a guess it would be this. Paul was so humbled and so remorseful that his zeal for God, before his conversion to Christianity, had caused him to actually torture and even to take part in the death of believers, all he wanted was a nod of approval from God. I believe he labored for that approval. He worked and suffered as few others have to obtain it. God told him early on that he was going to have to suffer great things in his life. And Paul willingly embraced that suffering in the hopes that when it was over, that he would not be considered a reprobate, but rather, that he would have done those things that made his life pleasing to God. For him, that was all the reward that was needed.

So, back to David. What was it that he was looking for? Well, we know that David had a heart for God. God even declared that to be so Himself when he spoke through the prophet Samuel to King Saul.

> **But now your kingdom will not endure;**
> **the LORD has sought out a man after**
> **his own heart and appointed him**
> **leader of his people ... (1 Sam. 13-14)**

He was speaking of David who was still just a shepherd boy in his father's home at that time. What was it about David that attracted God to him? You can discover that by looking into some of his writings. I think the gist of David's life before God can be summed up by the first 8 verses of Psalm 26.

> **... I have trusted in the LORD**

without wavering.
Test me, O LORD, and try me,
examine my heart and my mind;
for your love is ever before me,
and I walk continually in your truth.
I do not sit with deceitful men,
nor do I consort with hypocrites;
I abhor the assembly of evildoers
and refuse to sit with the wicked.
I wash my hands in innocence,
and go about your altar, O LORD,
proclaiming aloud your praise
and telling of all your wonderful deeds.
I love the house where you live, O LORD,
the place where your glory dwells.

In this Psalm we can discover two major insights. We can see how David attempted to conduct his life in order to improve his relationship with God, and we also see why he wanted to improve his relationship with God ... the reward he was after. In the first seven verses you can see how he conducted his life. "I do this ... I don't do that ... I do this ... I don't do that." These were the things that he believed God desired of him. But then in verse 8 he reveals his heart ... the heart that God saw and caused God to call him "a man after His own heart." He said,

I love the house where you live, O LORD,
the place where your glory dwells.

DECISIONS, DECISIONS, DECISIONS

David loved the Presence of God. There was nothing in the natural that David was not willing to do in order to dwell in or near the Presence of God. For him, if he could only find a way to remain in that Presence, that was all the reward he needed. All the struggles ... all the trials ... everything would be worth it. His love for that Presence was demonstrated again in 2 Samuel 6:14. It was the occasion of David and the Israelites bringing the Ark of the Covenant back to Jerusalem. The Ark represented the Presence of God. Look at David, keeping in mind that he was the king of that nation. It says:

> **David, wearing a linen ephod, danced**
> **before the LORD with all his might,**
> **while he and the entire house of**
> **Israel brought up the ark of the**
> **LORD with shouts and the sound**
> **trumpets. (2 Sam. 6:14-15)**

In another place it says that he leaped and danced. His exuberance was so great that it became undignified for a man of his position. When one of David's wives saw him, she was so embarrassed that she despised him in her heart. But David did not care. The Presence of God was his passion. He had all the reward he needed. He reiterated his consuming desire in the very next Psalm. It says:

> **One thing I ask of the LORD,**
> **this is what I seek:**

> that I may dwell in the house of the **LORD**
> all the days of my life,
> to gaze upon the beauty of the **LORD**
> and to seek him in his temple. (Ps. 27:4)

There was only one thing that David craved. That was to dwell in the house of the Lord. Why? Because in that day, that is where His Presence was. And although there are many verses that show David's desires for the Presence of God, Psalm 42 gives us as clear a picture of that passion as can be found anywhere.

> As the deer pants for streams of water,
> so my soul pants for you, **O God**.
> My soul thirsts for God, for the living **God**.
> When can I go and meet with **God**? (vs. 1-2)

"When can I go and meet with God?" That passion consumed him. It was the driving force of his life. If he could obtain it, all would have been worthwhile. And that has been the motivating factor behind many of the great men and women of God throughout history. They came to realize that there is no prize greater than the Presence of God. If that reward is obtainable, then there is no other reward. To them, anything else is a consolation prize.

I have had that hunger for many years myself. Lately though I have found fuel for my fire. Earlier in this writing I mentioned Tommy Tenney, and referred to him as a "God Chaser." Listen to me closely here.

DECISIONS, DECISIONS, DECISIONS

What I say about Mr. Tenney is not intended to elevate him in any way, and that is how he would want it. People in the pursuit of the Presence of God are not in pursuit of the accolades of man. But God gives different servants different insights and abilities. Their job is to share those with the body in general for the building up of the church. In his series of books pertaining to the pursuit of, the preparing for and the receipt of the manifest Presence of God, Tommy Tenney has helped me to see that that close personal intimacy with God is not only to be desired, but also to be attained. As I first opened the book, The God Chasers, I felt as though it was written to me. It was as though God was saying,

"I have seen you pursuing me for these years. I have seen you wonder if it was an attainable goal. I gave these insights to Tommy so that he could share them with you and others like you, whose primary drive in life is to find Me. I want you to find Me even more than you want it yourself ... and there are ways to do it. But there are some things that have to be, and others that can not be, if my Presence is to be manifest."

And after I read *The God Chasers,* I read *The God Catchers*, and then *God's Favorite House*. And by the time 3 weeks had passed I had read six of his books ... and I had pre-ordered *Finding Favor With the King*, and was waiting for its upcoming release. It is the story of how Esther prepared for her encounter with the king. And that is where my pursuit ran into the study of kairos moments. I began to realize that I wasn't paying enough attention to the small crossroads of my life. I wasn't making decisions that would lead me to that major encounter with God that I hungered for. And I certainly wasn't doing those things that were necessary to create the opportunity to have an encounter with God. I was not seeing to it that the things that the manifest Presence of God will not tolerate were eliminated from my life, nor was I actively incorporating the things He desires into my life.

Does that make it sound like I am doing "works" to obtain the Presence of God? I know that "works" have become a byword in this day. People are so afraid that they might transgress by appearing to be "working for their salvation" that they quit working entirely. But they err when they do that. Can you earn your salvation by works? No! It is the gift of God's Grace. But does your walk with God require work? Absolutely! We are commanded to "work out our own salvation with fear and trembling." We don't work *for* it, but we work out the details *of* it. We are commanded to take up our cross daily and to follow Christ. You can't take up a cross and not call it work. You can't be in the middle of fighting a spiritual warfare and not work. Warfare is work. We are also so entrenched in the idea of our salvation being "free" that we don't want to give up anything lest we be accused of trying to buy or earn our salvation. Is there any price that we could pay in order to receive salvation? No! But does it cost us anything? Yes! Not only does it cost us something .... it costs us everything. It costs us our lives and livelihood. It costs us our family and our friends. It costs us our positions in this life. It costs us our very lives. And I could give you scriptures to support everyone of those statements, but won't do so here. Serving God ... drawing close to Him will cost you everything. Does that mean that He will take everything away from us? No! But if we seek Him earnestly and He examines our hearts and finds that we are clinging to money or lands or family or friends or status ... or anything, He will not allow us into His Presence until we give those things up to Him. He has declared with His own mouth that He is a jealous God. If we truly want His Presence, we can't want anything else. Paul called it dung. Nothing in this world is to be compared with the Presence of God. It costs all we have ... and is worth more than that.

So what is the prize for seeking God so diligently that you go through life attempting to create kairos moments that might allow you to have an encounter with Him? Well, I still don't know. For Apostle Paul I think it was the hope of being called a faithful servant. For David, and Mr. Tenney it is the hope of spending eternity ... or a day ... or a moment in the Presence of God. Even a moment makes the effort of attaining it worthwhile. For Jesus I think it was to be obedient, even to the death on the cross. Yes, He will receive the Kingdom for His work, but I think that in His heart the reward came in knowing that He pleased the Father. But for you ... I can't answer the question. Only you can. The Word says that God creates desires within us. Desires to serve Him and to search for Him.

Then He puts within us the ability to attain those desires. So what are the desires of your heart toward God. If they are Godly desires, then that will be your primary reward for seeking Him more earnestly. He put those desires there in order for you to have something to work toward. The proverbial carrot dangling before the horse. There is nothing wrong with working for the reward ... especially when the reward is in God ... *or is God.*

CHAPTER 10

Personal Notes

In the course of my fifty-four years I have seen many kairos moments come and go. I did not recognize them by that name until recently, but they were there. Just like the event we talked about with Jesus and the Triumphal Entry, I have seen them come and go on a national level ... and you probably have too. Just as the nation of Israel failed to recognize the opportune time that was upon them with the birth of Jesus Christ, our nation has failed at many of its kairos moments in recent years. We have successfully navigated others.

When Israel declared its sovereignty in 1948 the United States faced a kairos. The Word of God says that He (God) will bless those who bless Israel and curse those who curse Israel. The United States took a stance at that time in support of Israel. We have, to a large extent, continued with that policy to this present time.

We initially navigated that kairos successfully and obtained the blessing of God. I pray that we continue to maintain that stance. I believe it is one of the few decisions we have made as a nation that has kept the judgment of God from falling upon us in a greater way than it has.

When the issue of prayer in our public schools came up in 1962 we failed a major kairos. We, in essence, told God that we were barring him from the education of our children. Well, in the years that have followed, Godlessness, immorality and violence have taken a dramatic increase. God will not abide where He is not welcome. If we don't want Him in our schools ... He won't stay in our schools. But after telling Him that He is not welcome there we can't reasonably expect Him to bless our children there ... or to protect them, physically or spiritually.

And, in 1964 the United States once again faced a major kairos. We were faced with making a decision about what we were going to do about racial prejudice as a nation. Was it going to continue to be the accepted norm, or would we take steps to give each man and woman ... each boy and girl equal standing and equal opportunity, with no regard for race or national origin? And although the implementation of the Civil Rights Act has been slow and arduous and filled with conflict, we made the Godly choice and passed that kairos.

When we came to the point of decision in the case of Roe v. Wade in 1973 we were at a kairos. When the Supreme Court of the United States ruled on that case and declared that a woman had the right to terminate the life of another human being we failed a kairos. It was not a ruling that the majority of the citizens of the United States wanted, but it became the law of the land because it was what the leadership of the courts wanted. God deals with individuals on an individual basis, but He also deals with nations on the basis of what the leaders of those nations do. The hand of God's judgment has been and will continue to be upon us as a nation and as individuals as long as we cling to laws that violate His laws.

At this very moment we face, as a nation, a kairos of major significance. It is not politically correct to view it in this way, but it is Biblically correct. States are now deciding, denominations are now deciding, and the nation will soon decide what to do about same-sex marriages. The correct decision is very plain, yet an ever-increasing number of people, including professing Christians, are deceived on the matter. God made it very clear in His Word. 1 Cor. 6:9 and following enumerates a long list of activities which are not acceptable in God's sight. Those verses even go on to state that people who practice such behavior will not be granted admittance into His Kingdom. There are those who wish it were some other way, but it is not. It will never be. In the Old Testament, God destroyed the region of Sodom and Gomorrah because of the stench sexual perversion put in His nostrils. It was His policy in the Old Testament; it was His policy in the New Testament, and it is His policy today. God does not change. But the point is that this nation stands at a major crossroad where we will deliberate passing laws that are major violations of God's laws. If we do, we will not go unpunished.

Can you see by looking back that those were and are major kairos points. Even if you do not agree with my assessment of which ones were successfully navigated and which ones were failed, you can still recognize them as crucial points in our history. That is what makes them kairos points. They were the points where we made decisions ... and our destiny was effected ... or determined.

Well, the same principle holds true at lower levels of organization and authority as well. In my life I have had the opportunity to see churches, as bodies, both pass kairos points in their church history, and also fail kairos moments in their history. One of the most notable success stories on which you can find documentation is with Sagemont Baptist Church in Houston, Texas. I was not part of that success story, but it is an absolutely awesome story of God getting involved in a church as a corporate entity because of the decisions of the leadership. The story is lengthy and I won't go into it here, but if you want to discover what making good and Godly decisions can mean in the life of a church, contact them and get audio tapes. You will be blessed.

Another success story based on good decisions would be with Lakewood Church, also in Houston. It was founded by the late John Osteen in 1959 in a converted feed store/barn type of structure. Under Pastor Osteen's Godly care and good decision making, it grew into one of the grandest churches in the United States. Then when Pastor Osteen passed away, decisions had to be made. Difficult decisions. His son Joel, whom I do not know personally (although I was an acquaintance of his father), would be the first to tell you that he had no ambitions or desires to be a pastor. He simply was not a preacher. Yet he did love God ... passionately. He did want to see the will of God fulfilled in his life. So he prayed. He came to a cross-road and found both Wisdom and Folly awaiting him ... wooing him. He asked God for Wisdom and God granted it. The results are now obvious. The church has exploded into what I believe is the largest church in the United States today. It is a tremendous example of church leadership successfully navigating a kairos.

Regrettably, I have had the opportunity to witness just the opposite results in churches as well. Why bring those up? Because it is not just the successes that make us want to choose well at our kairos'. It is a comparison between the results when good choices are made versus the results when poor choices are made. I will not, for obvious reasons, mention the names of the churches about which these observations were made, but there have been two of note. And I say "regrettably" because in one sense it is. It is regrettable for the leadership of those churches because they failed in the commission that God had given them to care for His flock. It is regrettable for the people of those churches because they will, as long as they remain there, be deprived of walking in places with God that would have been pleasant to them. Can they still reach deeper and more wonderful places in God as individuals? Absolutely! But the joy of that is different than the joy of going to magnificent places with God as a body of believers who love one another. They can't go there as a group unless the leadership of the church is willing and able to take them there.

The first instance involved a group of people who, for the most part, never even knew that a kairos came and went. A few people knew ... the leadership knew ... and God knew, because it was a day of His visitation. He heard the prayers of a very small percentage of the members of that church, and He visited them. Then some doctrinal issues arose, and from the pulpit the pastor declared that "this is what we believe." Well, what he stated as the "beliefs" denied the Holy Spirit a place to work in the midst of the congregation. The fervor that had built within the church died as quickly as if you had flipped a light switch. I don't have reason to hear about that church much, but last I heard it had continued to decline and God had not visited there in a significant way again. A truly sad example of how poor decisions at the leadership level can effect the outcome of a kairos in a church even though the people were hungry for God.

The other example, though, is even sadder. In this case almost the entire church had a hunger for God. The majority of the leadership was seeking a move of God. The people were seeking a move of God. And God had heard them. They had taken steps to create a kairos as a body. They had done what was needed in order to have a visitation from God. From week to week the air of excitement and anticipation grew until it seemed there had to be a climax of some sort. And when the moment of decision came, the leadership failed. They came right to the brink of a major break-through in the Kingdom of God. Their destiny was almost within their grasp. It was similar to the children of Israel and the Land of Canaan. The twelve spies went in to spy out the land. God was ready. The people were ready. But fear gripped the hearts of the majority of the spies. They knew they were not able to face the obstacles on their own, and they were not at a place in God where they had faith to trust His care.

And so it was with this case. The leadership saw the good things on the other side. But they also saw that the move of God was bigger than they were ready for. They saw that they could not lead the people there because it required going places in God that they had not been as individuals before. And the leadership of a church cannot lead the people to places where they, themselves, have not been. There might be cases where the leadership and the people could reach new and deeper places in God together if they both are willing to go there. But a church can't be led to places in God by leadership who has never been there. In this case, fear and pride gripped the leadership, and decisions were made that snuffed out the kairos. The last I heard, that church was in decline as well. And that is frequently how it is with a move of God. He visits once and moves on. He did it with Israel, although He will eventually visit there again. He visits nations and leaders once, and depending on what happens,

He may not ever visit again. And it is the same with individuals. And that is the point upon which I want to finish the body of this book.

God sees to it that as an individual, you will have kairos decisions to make concerning Him. The tendency on the part of many people is to put it off, especially with regard to making a decision about their personal salvation. The mindset is too frequently, "There is always tomorrow ... or when I am old." But that path has disaster at its end. You see, there are several things that keep that from being a sound decision. The first one is that the future is uncertain. Almost no one who dies suddenly is expecting it when it happens. We all expect to live to a ripe and good age. But that is all too frequently not the case. Jesus called the man a fool who said that he would build bigger barns for more of this world's goods and then sit back and enjoy life. His life was required of him that very day. Our days are in God's hands, not ours.

And then, even if we don't die prematurely, it is not always possible for us to turn to God for salvation. In order for us to come to Christ, God has to draw us as stated by Jesus himself in John 6:44.

> **No one can come to me unless the**
> **Father who sent me draws him...**

And while you might think that God will take you any time He can get you to come to Him, that is not true. He draws you and you either say yes or no. Look at the foreshadow of salvation in the Old Testament. It is actually written about in the New Testament in Hebrews 12:17, but it is speaking of Esau in the Old Testament.

> **For you know that afterward, when he wanted to inherit the blessing, he was rejected, for he found no place for repentance, though he sought it diligently with tears. (KJV)**

Esau wanted to repent, and sought it with tears, but it was not granted him. And then in 2 Tim. we read:

> **... in the hope that God will grant them repentance leading them to a knowledge of the truth, and that they will come to their senses and escape from the trap of the devil, who has taken them captive to do his will. (2 Tim. 2:25-26)**

You see, we can not just repent and turn to God unless He is willing to draw us and grant us a place of repentance. And this applies not only to salvation but also to the ability to enter into a more intimate relationship with Him. He will usually place a hunger for more of His Presence in a believer's heart at some point along the way, but He may never draw a second time. You might say, "But doesn't the Word say that whosoever will may come." Yes it does, but look at that word "will." In order for us to "will" or "want" to come to Him, He has to place a hunger or an urging in our heart.

DECISIONS, DECISIONS, DECISIONS

Coming to God is not part of the will of unregenerate mankind.

I guess that the reason these things are fresh in my spirit, and the reason my heart is tender toward them is because of where I am in my life right now. To help you understand that I will need to tell you a little about my life. Having been born in 1949, my high school years fell between 1964 and 1968. If you were alive then or have studied that time period, you know that it was one of the most tumultuous times in American history. As a teenager I was caught up fully in the cultural changes that swept our society at that time. I won't go into the depths of my depravity here, but just let me say that I was a much closer friend of Satan's than I was of God's. But do you remember me speaking of my family being intercessors? Well, part of the accomplishments of their intercession was to convince God to give me one more chance when I deserved no more chances. In fact I was standing at the gates of Hell when He gave me that chance. I had abused my body to the point that I hardly had a body ... or mind. But at Christmas of 1968, as a Christmas present to my Mother (it was what she asked for), I went to church. And there I received what I now believe would have been the last chance for me to find a place of repentance, and I came running to Christ. He drew me strongly ... powerfully ... and almost irresistibly. Tears track their way down my face at this moment, as I think about that moment. I had an encounter with the Presence of God that has never left me; nor has it left me unchanged.

After I finally made that one good choice at what was probably to have been my last kairos with God, I began to make other good choices. That very day I got together with all my Godless friends and witnessed to them about what God had done in my heart. Immediately after that I moved away to accomplish two things. I needed to get away from those friends in order to reduce the temptation to fall back into my old ways. And I needed to become grounded in the Word of God. I moved to Pensacola, Florida to attend Liberty Bible College.

Immediately upon enrolling, the principle that Jesus put forth concerning forgiveness became evident in my life. Jesus told us that whoever is forgiven much, loves much. And whoever is forgiven little, loves little. I was forgiven much ... and I was absolutely consumed with a passion for God and His Son. I pursued Him with a fervor at that time that still amazes me when I think about it today. Am I boasting when I write these things? No, because you haven't heard the shameful end to my story.

In short time God had begun to invest of His Spirit in my life. He enabled me to preach and share my testimony at conventions and "Jesus Rallies" (as they were called in those days). But they were meetings where youth, sometimes numbering in the thousands, would attend. And God would attend. And miracles would take place. And souls would be set free. And lives would be changed. And so wondrously did His hand work in my life that the thought of being prideful about it never entered my mind. In fact, it is only in looking back at it that I see the wonder of it all. But I was so young in the Lord. I had no idea at that time how special my visitation from God was. I just thought I was going through part of the normal routine of being a Christian. And because I did not recognize the magnificence of that kairos time in my life, I didn't treasure it. I didn't guard it. I didn't cultivate it. And it left me. And it has never returned in quite that way since.

Have I continued to serve God in the years that have passed since then? Yes. I have had ups and downs but no turnings back. There were years of that time when it was a struggle to just maintain a spiritual side of life at all. I did things and made decisions that not only brought disfavor with God, but also brought His judgment. But the work that He had done in me was deep; and even though I was way off course at times, I never looked at His correction in anger. I acknowledged my errors and thanked Him that He still loved me enough to correct me. I made up my mind that if He never spoke to me in an intimate way again, I would go to my grave thanking Him for the Grace He had extended me in my life. What I had already experienced of Him was greater than a mortal human being ought to be entitled to. And when I took that stance His Presence began to return in an intimate way. He began to show me that that all consuming longing that I had for Him in my heart could be satisfied. And the last dozen years or so have been wonderful in that regard. Has the power of His Spirit that once visited me returned? Not yet. But the hope of it ... the promise of it ... the possibility of it, has returned. And learning about kairos moments has been a big part of that.

I now realize that my original failure so many years ago was not so much a sin as it was a failure to recognize the time of His visitation in my life ... so He moved on. It has taken these thirty-plus years to even approach another kairos moment of that magnitude in my life. Have those years been wasted? No. They have been learning, growing years. But could they have been spent to greater profit for the Kingdom of God, and for my laying up of treasures in Heaven for myself? Sadly, yes.

You see, the Word says that before the world ever began, God established some steps and paths for me to walk on. He also determined some works for me to do and some blessings for me to partake in. We don't know what those blessings and paths and works consist of until we get to them. They are the exciting discoveries that we encounter as we make good decisions regarding the kairos' of our lives. In his very insightful book entitled, When God is First, Mike Hayes, Pastor of Covenant Church, Carrollton (Dallas), Texas, relates a story of a discussion he had with his son, Stephen. In the account, Covenant Church wanted to acquire a piece of undeveloped land in that very highly developed area of North Dallas. As they drove by the property, Stephen asked, "Dad, how long has this land been here?" Pastor Hayes looked at his son, pondered for a moment, and finally said, "Well Stephen, I guess God's been saving it for us since creation." The story is much more detailed when you read it in his book, and you should. Covenant Church now sits on forty acres of that property, has a physical facility far in excess of $20,000,000 and a lively membership of around twelve thousand. But the point as far as this book is concerned is this. Pastor Hayes and the leadership of Covenant Church did not have to encounter the opportunity to purchase that property. They got to that major kairos by having successfully created/navigated kairos' earlier in their history. A poor decision here ... an uncommitted act there ... a failure somewhere else ... and all their remaining kairos' moments could have been encountered in their smaller facility on the other side of Interstate 35.

I now realize a couple of things that urge me on in my pursuit. First, God established some things at the foundation of the world that He would have liked for me to walk in ... and He has done the same for you. The decisions we make early on determine if we are to ever encounter those great kairos', or if we will have to settle for smaller ones. If I had made different decisions at my earlier kairos moments, I would have encountered some blessings that I will now never see, because now, more than thirty years later, many of those have come and gone and are no longer accessible. They are lost to me, and my heart breaks over the fact that Jesus gave His all for me, and I have failed to fulfill His plans for my life. But the second thing that I now realize, and take great comfort in, is this. God is a God of Wondrous Grace. No, I can not go back and walk in those earlier paths, but He can visit me where I am and bring me to other kairos moments ... different than the others but just as wonderful. I want to walk in those paths. I want to encounter those kairos'. I want to walk in every good and Godly and powerful blessing that God will allow me to walk in for the remainder of my days on this Earth.

And that is where I am as I write this book. My days are filled with a consuming desire to be renewed in His Presence. I am somewhere between what it appears to me that David and Paul were looking for. I long for His Presence because it stirs my heart ... it is THE PRIZE. But I also want to do something for the Kingdom of God. Not to try to work my way into that Kingdom, but as a means of saying "thank you" to God, and to His Son for extending me the Grace and Mercy to be a part of that Kingdom. I have been unproductive for far too many of those years since I was first visited by God. The longing for His Presence is for my own enjoyment, but the longing to be given an assignment, and to accomplish that assignment is for both Him and me. You see, I know that Jesus Christ is about to receive His Kingdom. My heart cries out to be allowed to do something in that Kingdom. I want to do it for Him as a means of saying "thank you" for what He has done in my life. And I guess I need it for me so that I, like Paul, can be more comfortable in the knowledge that He has not only forgiven me for my shortcomings (and I am secure and comfortable in that knowledge), but that He has also re-included me in His plans. I slighted a monumental kairos in my life. Will I get another? Only God knows. The one I already had is more than I deserved. But I have made up my mind ...

DECISIONS, DECISIONS, DECISIONS

I have set a course ... I have begun to look, and will continue to look, for ways to create small kairos moments in my life that I believe will lead me to one more big kairos in my Earthly walk. It is the desire of my heart, and I rest in the assurance of His Word, where Jesus Himself said that those who seek Him would find Him ... and that if we draw near to Him, He will draw near to us. I get out of bed every day of my life expecting that one more life changing kairos with the God of the Universe.

Friends, kairos moments are paramount in this life. The Jews failed to recognize one in their nation about two thousand years ago. It broke Jesus' heart. I, like they, failed to recognize one about thirty years ago, and while it was not of the magnitude of the other, I suspect it still broke His heart. I failed to recognize mine out of ignorance, but I can no longer claim that as an excuse. And after having read this book, your level of accountability will never be the same either. Whenever we receive light we are held accountable for it. This book has opened my eyes to some things that I had never considered before, and I believe it has done the same thing inside you.

We will either incorporate these insights into our daily lives, or at some point we will have to explain to Him why we didn't. The potential is there. May we never again overlook the time of His visitation in our lives ... and even better yet, may we be ever looking for ways to create those times of visitation.

CHAPTER 11

The Final Kairos
(Or the Post Rapture Chapter)

The soul of this book has come to me through pondering the disasters in my life. In times past I have made strings of poor decisions which kept me perpetually heading down the wrong road, and eventually I would crash in a "near fatal" experience. A number of these crashes were near fatal in a physical sense of the word. As I sit here thinking of them and counting, I run out of fingers counting just the ones that I believe to be truly "close encounters of the death kind." And who knows how many I, or any of us, have been spared from, totally unaware of the protection of the angels of God? And those physical events were painful ... some excruciating. But there were other wrecks in my life as well. There have been emotional crashes, and spiritual ones. And a couple of times there were combinations of all three of them at the same time. The pain of the simply physical disasters is minute in comparison to the combination crashes. These are the sort that you can read about in the Psalms when David seemed near death from anguish of soul. God loved, and still loves, David with a special love. But that didn't spare him from reaping the consequences of sin. In fact, it only ensured his correction, because God chastens every child that He loves. So when David sinned he had a spiritual wreck. If the wreck came about as a result of God judging his sin there was also a physical disaster involved. And if people he loved, such as his son Absalom, were involved, then there was an emotional disaster also. All three of them coming at the same time can cause an anguish of soul such as a mortal man can barely sustain. And that anguish of soul can be seen, or heard, or felt, as David cries out to God for deliverance in some of his heart rending writings. Psalm 6:6-7 is only one of a multitude of examples.

> **I am worn out from groaning;**
> **all night long I flood my bed with weeping**
> **and drench my couch with tears.**
> **My eyes grow weak with sorrow;**
> **they fail because of all my foes.**

And, unless I miss my guess, David and I are not the only ones to have ever experienced these crushing disasters in life.

This book is being written toward the end of the year 2003. Daily, the news has stories about the fear of a flu pandemic. There are flu outbreaks around the world every year, but some are worse than others. Some are more deadly and more resistant. Some just seem to hang on and hang on. And while I don't mean to belittle anyone's flu episode, because they are all miserable, I am a veteran of the Asian flu pandemic in 1957-1958. It was a particularly virulent strain and resulted in over seventy thousand deaths in the United States alone. Even though I was only eight years old, I remember it well, and it provided me with a saying I have used many times in my life. My mom and dad, my two brothers and I all had the flu at the same time. We all ran fevers that were life threatening. We all were ridding our bodies of life sustaining liquids and electrolytes at a far faster pace than what we were able to put (and keep) them in our bodies. And we all had it at the same time. My parents did all they could to take care of us boys, and while I suspect that the three of us would have died without their care, the truth is that they were in no position to give us the care they would have liked to because they were so effected themselves. And like that last sentence, our affliction went on and on and on. Now, when an affliction or disaster comes my way and just seems to hang on, I think of that flu episode, and too many times I have referred to the trials of life as being "like the flu." What I mean by that is that life is such that I just feel like dying, and it goes on and on and on, and seems like it will never end. So while you may have never been through any of the truly devastating flu pandemics, I suspect that you have been through a disaster in life that was so crushing, so oppressive, so heart rending ... and so unending that it seemed as if you might not live through it ... and you might not have even wanted to.

But there is a day coming upon this planet which will give untold millions of people the gut wrenching feeling that I have just described. An awareness will have crept into each of them ... an awareness that they have failed the greatest kairos in the history of mankind. A feeling will flood them that disaster has struck and there is no escape. And while there actually will be a means of escape, the process will be so difficult, so monumental, so lengthy that they will think it will never end, though they may wish constantly that it would end, even at the cost of death. That moment will be when the Christians in the world are taken up into heaven in the rapture. Although there are debates over exactly when that event will occur, we are going to assume, for the sake of this discussion, that it occurs sometime, any time, before the actual second coming of Christ and the Millennial reign. This final chapter is written particularly to those persons who have found themselves left behind after that event.

If you are reading this book, and people you once categorized as religious ... or fanatical ... or Christian have been taken out of the world, you must be facing the darkest day of your existence. Feelings of absolute hopelessness have overwhelmed you and you have a sinking feeling in your heart that is greater than any you have ever felt before. You are absolutely certain that you have made the ultimate, and unfixable mistake. But I want to dedicate these last few pages to instructing you about a few things. The first of which is this. You have not made the ultimate mistake. Many millions of people before you have made that "final" or "ultimate" mistake, and millions more will make it soon. But you have not made it yet. Those who have made that error ... those who have no hope remaining ... those for whom there is no remedy, are those who failed at their critical kairos and then died without taking the steps to rectify their poor choices. You, on the other hand, have not died. You still have one remaining opportunity ... one kairos ... as long as you are still alive. Pay attention to what I have just said ... as long as you are still alive. The fact that you are alive right now means that you still have a chance to live forever. You still have a chance to join those that were recently taken out of your world. Let's look at that world.

You may have been a "doubter" in times past. You may have even ridiculed or scoffed about the religious fanatics you once knew. It may be that the only way you have ever used the name "Jesus" or "God" has been in a profane or disparaging way. But recent events have proven that you were wrong. And if you are to capitalize on the one opportunity you have remaining, that is where you have to begin ... by realizing, and by admitting that you were wrong. And you may not have long to make that admission. As times have worsened throughout the world there will have been many deaths by various means. Starvation, earthquake, unusual diseases, natural disasters, war and terrorism will have taken considerable toll on human population. But the worst is yet to come.

I have to believe that if you are one of those to

whom this chapter is written, not only are you reading this book, but you have found a Bible and are reading it as well. Take that Bible and open it to the seventh chapter of the Book of Revelation. You will see two or three things mentioned there that I have alluded to. First I want you to take note of the vast crowd that is gathered around the throne of God. The Bible says that the crowd was so great that no one could number it. Then one of the elders in heaven with whom John was conversing asked, "These in white robes-who are they, and where did they come from?" John said that he didn't know; so the elder told him. He said that the huge crowd was composed of those who had come out of the great tribulation. That verse can be talking about you. You can be one of those that washes your robe in the blood of the lamb. You can be one of those about whom it says,

> "they are before the throne of God
> and serve him day and night in his temple;
> and he who sits on the throne will spread
> his tent over them.
> Never again will they hunger;
> never again will they thirst.
> The sun will not beat upon them,
> nor any scorching heat.
> For the Lamb at the center of the
> throne will be their shepherd;
> he will lead them to springs of living water.
> And God will wipe away every tear
> from their eyes." (Rev. 7:15-17)

Your guts are wrenching now. Your heart is broken. You have wept until your eyes don't seem to have any more water. But there is still time to put yourself in position to have God wipe every last tear from your eyes forever. This book is about kairos moments, and this may be your last. An uncountable multitude is in the process of facing their final kairos even as you read this. Many will respond well ... others will not. We can see that even though a vast number will make their way to heaven by means of that one final successful kairos decision, others are set to make their final fatal mistake. Even though I showed you the verse in chapter 7 that offers hope, there are other verses that show that not everyone in the Tribulation will take advantage of their chance ... and others will not even get a chance. Chapter 6 talks a little about those people.

> When the Lamb opened the second seal,
> I heard the second living creature
> say, "Come!" Then another horse came
> out, a fiery red one. Its rider was given
> power to take peace from the earth and
> to make men slay each other. To him
> was given a large sword. When the
> Lamb opened the third seal, I heard the
> third living creature say, "Come!" I
> looked, and there before me was a
> black horse! Its rider was holding a
> pair of scales in his hand. Then I heard
> what sounded like a voice among the

> four living creatures, saying, "A quart
> of wheat for a day's wages, and three
> quarts of barley for a day's wages, and
> do not damage the oil and the wine!"
> When the Lamb opened the fourth
> seal, I heard the voice of the fourth
> living creature say, "Come!" I looked,
> and there before me was a pale horse!
> Its rider was named Death, and Hades
> was following close behind him. They
> were given power over a fourth of the
> earth to kill by sword, famine and
> plague, and by the wild beasts of the
> earth. (Rev. 6:3-8)

In these verses we have two events taking place. I won't take time to expound the entire Book of Revelation, but I will say a few things. What takes place in these verses is the beginning of disasters upon the earth. In verses 3 - 4 peace is taken from the earth and men begin to kill each other in huge numbers. This will most likely be in the form of terrorism. We are seeing the seeds for that beginning to sprout even now before the Tribulation, but it will increase, and life will become extremely uncertain. Then in verses 7 - 8 we have a separate event beginning. This is where supernatural things begin to occur which will take the lives of one fourth of the population of the earth. So between the deaths of the multitude that no one could count around the throne of God, and the multitudes that were killed for reasons other than serving God, the population of Earth will diminish quickly. You need to know that the entire time frame for the Tribulation is only seven years, so all of these deaths will occur rapidly. You may not have long. In fact, you can't have long. You could have at most seven years, but it is likely much less. Don't miss your moment. And this very moment could be "that" moment.

It is not the goal of this book to expound to any degree on the Book of Revelation. Just know that if you have found yourself in a somewhat vacated world, and have decided it was the Rapture of the Church that caused it, time is short. Over one half of the population of the world has recently, or will soon die. The odds of you surviving long are small. You have not missed your final kairos yet, but it may be at the door. If you read this and feel any favorable stirrings in your spirit at all toward God, you still have a chance. That stirring is His way of saying that He is giving you one more opportunity to find a place of soul saving repentance. Don't fail to recognize this last kairos. Read in 2 Cor. where it says:

> **... "In the time of my favor I heard you,**
> **and in the day of salvation I helped you."**
> **I tell you, now is the time of God's favor,**
> **now is the day of salvation. (2 Cor. 6:2)**

If God is stirring your heart, He is offering you one more chance. It is late, but not too late. You have one remaining kairos in your life. This is it. Allow me to help you enter it successfully. All that is necessary is for you to acknowledge some things in your heart, and to confess some things with your mouth. First, from your heart, you need to acknowledge that you have been wrong all your life. Your attitude toward God has been such that you deserve His judgment, which is eternity in Hell. You also need to acknowledge in your heart, that you now see your errors and that you now realize that Jesus is the Son of God. Read the New Testament if you need to in order to see that He came to Earth to pay the price for your sins and errors. Because He lived a sinless life, His sacrifice was perfect, and He made a way for anyone who believes to be restored to God. His righteousness, or perfectness, can apply to your sins if you confess him to be your Lord and Savior. If you believe that He was the Son of God, that He came to Earth and died for the sins of mankind, that He was resurrected from the dead, and that His sacrifice will cleanse you from your sins (not because you deserve it but because God is Gracious and Merciful), then you can be saved.

Believe these things in your heart and then go and tell them to someone you know. The Scriptures say that it is with our heart that we believe and are justified, and it is with our mouth that we confess and are saved. If you can do these things you will have passed the most important kairos that a human will ever encounter.